William Bartlett, Jadranka Bozikov and Bernd Rechel (*editors*)
HEALTH REFORMS IN SOUTH EAST EUROPE

Kevin Featherstone, Dimitris Papadimitriou, Argyris Mamarelis, Georgios Niarchos
THE LAST OTTOMANS
The Muslim Minority of Greece 1941–1949

Alexis Heraclides
THE GREEK-TURKISH CONFLICT IN THE AEGEAN
Imagined Enemies

Markus Ketola
EUROPEANIZATION AND CIVIL SOCIETY
Turkish NGOs as instruments of change?

New Perspectives on South-East Europe
Series Standing Order ISBN 978–0–230–23052–1 (hardback) and
ISBN 978–0–230–23053–8 (paperback)

You can receive future titles in this series as they are published by placing a standing order. Please contact your bookseller or, in case of difficulty, write to us at the address below with your name and address, the title of the series and the ISBNs quoted above.

Customer Services Department, Macmillan Distribution Ltd, Houndmills, Basingstoke, Hampshire RG21 6XS, England

---

Europeanization and Civil Society

Turkish NGOs as instruments of change?

Markus Ketola
*Fellow in Social Policy and Development, Department of Social Policy,
London School of Economics and Political Science, UK*

First published 2013 by
PALGRAVE MACMILLAN

Palgrave Macmillan in the UK is an imprint of Macmillan Publishers Limited, registered in England, company number 785998, of Houndmills, Basingstoke, Hampshire RG21 6XS.

Palgrave Macmillan in the US is a division of St Martin's Press LLC, 175 Fifth Avenue, New York, NY 10010.

Palgrave Macmillan is the global academic imprint of the above companies and has companies and representatives throughout the world.

Palgrave® and Macmillan® are registered trademarks in the United States, the United Kingdom, Europe and other countries.

ISBN 978–1–137–03451–9

This book is printed on paper suitable for recycling and made from fully managed and sustained forest sources. Logging, pulping and manufacturing processes are expected to conform to the environmental regulations of the country of origin.

A catalogue record for this book is available from the British Library.

A catalog record for this book is available from the Library of Congress.

To Rachel

Contents

List of Figures and Boxes

Acknowledgements

Any acknowledgements can only be the start of a long, long list of people who have helped me on the journey of writing this book. A significant part of the research has been based on interviews with practitioners working for NGOs, government and the EU Delegation to Turkey. Their stories and experiences are an absolutely essential element of this research project and my first thanks is to those who often took considerable time out of their busy schedules to meet with me. It is my hope that their views and comments are accurately reflected in the pages that follow (although the responsibility for any shortcomings and errors is of course mine).

At LSE, Jude Howell, Hakan Seckinelgin, Armine Ishkanian and David Lewis all played their part in helping me refine the arguments found here, and I would like to thank them for the interesting discussions about civil society, NGOs, Turkey and other issues touched upon in the book. My friends in Turkey also deserve a special mention for the hospitality and support they showed during my several research visits. In particular I would like to thank Alex Massavetas, Cihan Tutluoğlu, Levent and Güllü Bingöl, Aysu Katun, Senem Erberk, Erçin Ural and Reeta Paakkinen. I would also like to thank Engin Akcay in Ankara and Celil Kaya in Diyarbakir for helping me with several of the key interviews.

Saving the best for last, I want to thank Rachel from the bottom of my heart for the support she has shown and for her patience when I was trying to complete this work. Because of these reasons (and many more) the book is dedicated to her.

List of Acronyms

ADD	Association for Kemalist Thought
AKP	Justice and Development Party
AP	Justice Party
CFCU	Central Finance and Contracts Unit
CHP	Republican People's Party
CSO	Civil Society Organization
CSDC	Civil Society Development Centre
ÇYDD	Association for the Support of Modern Life
DEHAP	Democratic People's Party
DİSK	Revolutionary Labour Unions Confederation of Turkey
DoA	Department of Associations
DP	Democrat's Party
DTP	Democratic Society Party
EC	European Commission
EU	European Union
EUROCHAMBRES	European Association of Chambers of Commerce and Industry
EUSG	Turkish Secretariat General for EU Affairs
HADEP	People's Democracy Party
HAK-İŞ	Confederation of Turkish Just Workers' Union
İKV	Economic Development Foundation
IMF	International Monetary Fund
KESK	Confederation of Public Workers' Unions
KKK	Kurdistan Workers Party
MEMUR-SEN	Confederation of Public Servants' Union
MHP	Nationalist Action Party

MİSK	Nationalist Labour Union's Confederation
MSP	National Salvation Party
NGO	Non-Governmental Organization
NPM	New Public Management
NSC	National Security Council
RP	Islamist Welfare Party
THK	Turkish Aeronautical Association
TİSK	Turkish Confederation of Employers' Unions
TOBB	Turkish Union of Chambers and Commodities Exchanges
TÜRK-İŞ	Confederation of Turkish Trade Unions
TÜSİAD	Turkish Industrialists' and Businessmen's Association
TVYD	Television Broadcasters' Association
TZOB	Turkish Union of Agricultural Chambers
WB	World Bank

1
Introduction

Civil society plays an intrinsic part in the European Union (EU) enlargement process, making Turkish civil society an important actor in Turkey's pre-accession process for EU membership. This book aims to capture some of the main characteristics of this relationship between the EU and Turkish non-governmental organizations (NGOs),[1] and in so doing develops the following overarching argument. First of all, EU civil society policy, by its very nature, employs an external agenda for reform that rarely accommodates the nature of the domestic socio-political environment. Secondly, NGOs do not passively accept this agenda but operate as autonomous agents, often circumventing and resisting the aims and objectives of the externally conceived programme of civil society support. As such, the book intends to highlight the importance of informal domestic rules and norms that determine how NGOs choose to internalize the agenda introduced by EU civil society policy. Ultimately this interplay between the external and internal means that the outcomes of EU civil society funding in Turkey are inherently unpredictable.

In the current phase of the process, Turkey and the EU have engaged in a period of 'harmonization' where Turkey is committed to adopting the *acquis*[2] of the European Union. In other words, Turkey is facing a momentous process of change as it executes the required policy reforms. The role envisaged for civil society has much to do with an increased engagement in the policymaking arena, and as such civil society initiatives have largely concentrated on NGOs. The underlying expectations suggest that NGOs can facilitate the reform process by offering an avenue for dialogue with the public as well as an alternative party to be consulted during policymaking. Conceptually, this kind of behaviour by NGOs links up with notions of change that have been captured by the terms 'Europeanization' and 'democratization'.

But how does such a vision relate to Turkish civil society that is both culturally and historically different from European civil societies? For some observers civil society in Turkey exists more in quantity than in quality (Şimşek, 2004, p. 252; Kalaycıoğlu, 2004), referring to the fact that even though, numerically speaking, Turkish civil society has developed tremendously, the behaviour of civil society actors has been such that the qualitative impact on the processes of democratization and Europeanization remains limited. At the same time civil society has been identified as a key arena where both of these processes are expected to unfold (Göle, 1994; Keyman and Öniş, 2007; Keyman and Icduygu, 2003; Kubicek, 2005; Tocci, 2005). It is the apparent disconnect between the importance attached to civil society in theoretical and policymaking terms as an engine of transformative processes and the practical limitations for civil society to effectively manage this role that is of concern here. Does civil society in Turkey generate the kind of response that the Europeanization and democratization policies expect?

The chapters in this book engage with these questions. The relationship between the EU and Turkish civil society is poised between two sets of interests that possess an air of incommensurability. For the EU, Turkish civil society is one of the means to exact change required by the EU accession process. This policy of Europeanization, which aims at meeting accession conditions such as full compliance with the EU *acquis*, is realized through a unidirectional set of requirements that reflects the bureaucratic demands of 'EUization' and pays less attention to the reality of NGO existence on the ground Diez, Agnantopoulos and Kaliber, 2005, p. 2).

Turkish NGOs, however, are not passive recipients of these policies. Domestic pressures and issues interweave with the opportunities brought about by EU funding. Precisely because a gap exists between the EU and NGO expectations, the latter are compelled to search for locally meaningful responses to the opportunities and challenges that EU funding poses. NGOs expect their contribution to be taken seriously, in the sense of being more than mere vehicles that can be used to complete projects. They expect to be treated more as equal partners who bring something unique to the partnership and should have more influence in determining the 'what' and 'how' elements of projects. Their reactions are determined by these expectations together with the domestic political context. Whether NGOs deem these expectations to be met is at least partly determined by the capacity of the NGO to rise to the challenge of managing EU-funded projects. Under these circumstances, civil society actors generate a variety of reactions and responses. This point of view offers a different way of understanding Europeanization as a local process where the EU-led practices are internalized by domestic actors in their modes of operation. In this way Europeanization can unfold differently from 'intended Europeanization' (Ioakimidis, 2001, p. 74), spawning unintentional consequences as local actors attach different meanings and understandings to the processes of change they are witnessing.

The book aims at understanding how these differences materialize and how they are negotiated. It does so through a series of interviews with civil society activists, EU bureaucrats and Turkish officials who have been involved in the EU funding processes, exploring how civil society actors behave and why certain practices occur. This research scrutinizes the tension that inevitably exists between the need to design broad policy objectives and the everyday practices of the recipients of such policies. The new systems that are introduced by these policies – the system of EU civil society funding being the focus here – need to be (and are being) internalized and mediated before they acquire meaning at the local level. This understanding places certain conditions on and limitations to what can be achieved by an externally designed policy intervention.

The primary focus of this study is NGOs that work on rights-based issues, such as human rights, women's rights, youth rights and child rights. The majority of the organizations researched in the context of this book have been advocacy NGOs, working on such rights-based issues and located in Istanbul, Ankara and Diyarbakir: the three main hubs of EU civil society funding.

Europeanization

As others have observed, Europeanization is not a theory in itself. Rather it is a phenomenon, a puzzle that requires explanation (Graziano and Vink, 2008; Radaelli, 2004). Thus, using the aforesaid arguments to make sense of EU–NGO relations in Turkey leads to a particular explanation of what is meant by Europeanization. There are three broad perspectives. First, at its broadest, Europeanization alludes to the relationship between norms, policies, rules and regulations that exist at the European level, and those that are present at the national level. This type of Europeanization is often cited in the context of EU accession negotiations, referring to a top-down process in which EU directives and policies are being adopted by nation states (Kazamias and Featherstone, 2001). Second, and alternatively, Europeanization can be seen as a process of domestic pressures feeding into the decisions of national actors, which in turn may guide the forms of governance at the European level. These two sources of influence are likely to interact, working as a two-way process that determines the final form Europeanization takes (Kazamias and Featherstone, 2001, p. 6). Third, Europeanization can be seen as a purely domestic process, where local actors, local problems and local discourse engage with European variables, and where the outcomes feed directly back into the domestic environment (Radaelli, 2004). The key point of difference here is that domestic reactions are not purely reactions to European influences. What is common to all three perspectives, something inherent in the very word Europeanization, is the underlying focus on change.

Each of these three perspectives retains some relevance to the case of EU civil society funding in Turkey. EU funding is anchored to the Copenhagen Criteria, which set forth the political, economic and policy requirements for all new member states and form the backbone of a top-down, technical process of Europeanization. At the same time the NGOs that receive EU funding are embedded in and informed by the domestic political and cultural practices. The pressures and influences that derive from the local context feed into the decisions NGOs make within the funding framework. Finally, NGO behaviour spills over to areas that cannot be understood solely by reference to EU-imposed Europeanization or by NGO reactions to Europeanization-related policies. NGOs are able to operate in a variety of ways, utilizing EU funding and other normative forms of Europeanization in their domestic activities, yet without outcomes that may be considered explicitly Europeanizing.

Given that the book is concerned primarily with the behaviour of the actors on the ground and their responses to Europeanization processes in Turkey, the study aligns with 'sociological institutional-ism' (also called constructivist institutionalism). This is one of the three 'new institutionalist' approaches that are frequently applied to the study of Europeanization within European Studies (Kazamias and Featherstone, 2001; Eilstrup-Sangiovanni, 2006; Schimmelfennig and Sedelmeier, 2008).[3] Sociological institutionalism emphasizes the importance of the informal rules and norms that influence decision-making. When an institution influences the behaviour of actors, this is not simply down to a threat of sanctions or conditionalities that may have been imposed. These actors must internalize the responsi-bilities placed upon them by the institution. It is a question of social-ization, whereby actors internalize the new rules and norms. This in turn affects how they see their interests (Eilstrup-Sangiovanni, 2006, p. 395). Similarly, Diez (1999) describes Europeanization as an enabling concept, not as something that causes things directly. It energizes actors to act by creating certain conditions, but it does not prescribe a certain way of behaving. The decisions made by the actors involved ultimately determine the outcomes of Europeanization. The structures of European integration and Europeanization are not rigid but vague.

Donors and civil society

The focus on NGOs forms a subfield within civil society studies, looking at particular types of formal organizations that operate within the civil societal space, whose work often resonates strongly with donor objectives. The relationship between the EU and Turkish civil society can be best described as a variant of the donor–NGO relationship that is widely discussed in the literature on civil soci-ety. One defining element of these relationships is the existence of a facility for providing financial support. Quite often the growth of the NGO sector has been supply-driven, meaning that the organi-zations do not necessarily arise out of local needs and may not be the most suitable for the needs and requirements of the country in question (Ottaway and Carothers, 2000, p. 299). Donor priorities shift frequently, forcing NGOs to realign their interests in order to compete for funding (Howell and Pearce, 2001b). Yet, chasing the money trail may have a negative impact on the ability of advocacy NGOs to retain a reputation for independence, a quality that is considered a key ingredient in being able to influence a political process (Bratton, 1989; Edwards and Hulme, 1996; Hulme and Edwards, 1997; Ottaway and Carothers, 2000; Parks, 2008). The supply-driven nature of donor funding leads one to question what exactly is being achieved with the help of these funds, and how this relates to the stated aims of donor-funded programmes.

Democratization, often in connection with human rights initiatives, has become a critical part of the civil society funding rationale for international donor organizations. Within the conventional neo-Tocquevillean views of civil society (a theme Chapter 3 elaborates on), greater civil society activism is likely to lead to more accountable governance, more effective policy implementation and democratic reform (Mercer, 2002). The existence of civil society in itself is therefore taken as a positive sign of democratic development (Diamond, 1994; Putnam, Leonardi and Nanetti, 1994). It is labelled as 'good' and becomes conceptually distinct from the 'bad' state and market (Bebbington, Hickey and Mitlin, 2008, p. 6). Carothers (1997) points to a duality of purpose behind democracy promotion by donors. On the one hand, democratization is seen as an end in itself; it brings freedom and governmental accountability which will improve people's lives. On the other hand, democracy is good for social and economic development and is therefore regarded as one component of a successful development programme. This latter purpose, Carothers suggests, has been more prevalent in donor programmes in Africa, where economic issues have taken priority (cf. Crawford, 1997, 2001). Policies aiming for democratization, therefore, tend to interlace with social and economic aims.

These kinds of donor efforts to engage NGOs have been criticized for being estranged from the political realities of the local context and civil society. Local civil society is, after all, the domain within which funded NGOs operate. Subsequent donor support instrumentalizes civil society, making it the means to an end, not an end in itself. This erodes the political edge of civil society as it becomes a vehicle for delivering goals conceived by the donors (Howell and Pearce, 2001a), and as Bebbington, Hickey and Mitlin observe, 'NGOs are only NGOs in any politically meaningful sense of the term if they are offering alternatives to dominant models, practices and ideas about development' (2008, p. 3). What is more, the donor goals often assume an air of universality, purporting a particular package of moral values and organizational forms as the only one available. Civil society becomes confined within the Western model of liberal individualism (Hann and Dunn, 1996, p. 3), a context in which the ideas of NGOs and projects become reified as the vehicle through which change can be delivered (Howell and Pearce, 2001b). Civil society has been 'dusted off and deodorized to suit a variety of ideological, intellectual and practical needs' (White, 1994, p. 370). Has civil society, as Chandhoke suggests, been a victim of its own success, where popularity has made it an overly consensual and flattened concept (2001), leading to overly superficial and generic donor strategies (Carothers, 1997)? These questions and concerns highlight the need for a different approach. Mindful of this, others consider civil society as a site of 'struggle, multivocality and paradox' (Glasius, Lewis and Seckinelgin, 2004, p. 10) and emphasize the need to pay careful attention to the informal and interpersonal practices present in civil society (Hann and Dunn, 1996).

In other words, the reward of EU membership is contingent on the fulfilment of a long list of reforms. In comparison to the kind of donor–NGO relationship that is described in much of the literature (Mercer, 2002; Howell and Pearce, 2001a; Carothers, 2004), the relationship in Turkey, given the broader context of Europeanization and EU accession, has processes attached that are not present elsewhere. While the formal funding procedures are unidirectional (the EU determines project aims and decides on monitoring criteria), there are numerous opportunities for civil society actors to internalize and mediate the system of funding so that it gains meaning in the local context. In this way, the actor-oriented perspective offers interesting insights to the role played by civil society in this context. Furthermore, the impact of EU funding is not limited to those CSOs that receive funding. It also has an effect on the behaviour of civil society actors who are unable or refuse to apply for funding. Given the existence of such conditioning factors, the funding operation ultimately has uncertain outcomes. A complex web of interactions and responses arise from these dynamics and pull in various directions, making the outcomes of Europeanization unpredictable.

Structure of the book

Following the introductory comments made here, Chapter 2 visits the theories of civil society, outlining the main theoretical strands that help to explain not only the nature of civil society in Turkey but also the current debates that form the basis of the logic behind EU policies towards civil society. The chapter seeks to determine whether Western theoretical frameworks remain relevant when explaining what is taking place in Turkey and suggests that the way in which EU policy – grounded in Western frameworks of thinking about civil society – projects a range of normative assumptions onto Turkey differs greatly from the reality of civil society on the ground.

Chapter 3 delves deeper into the logic and motivations behind the EU's interest in engaging with civil society actors in Turkey. By tracing through the chronology of policy documents that outline EU policy over the past 20 years, this chapter shows that the overall policy applied within the EU, in Turkey as well as in the broader Mediterranean, stems from the same logic that reflects an instrumental understanding of the role of civil society (i.e. it can be a vehicle for other policy goals), and a universal understanding of what is meant by civil society (i.e. civil society is more or less the same despite different cultural and historical contexts).

Chapter 4 presents an analysis of the evolution of Turkish civil society and captures the unique and idiosyncratic characteristics of civil society in the Turkish context. The historical linkage between civil society and the political project of secularization led to a bifurcation between secular civil society that functioned as the bulwark for the Turkish state, and the rest of civil society (representing, for example, religious and minority interests) that did not fit as comfortably within the secular mould. These divisions are sustained by NGOs, through the vociferous debate that is often carried out in essentialist terms. The absence of compromises, in turn, questions the ability of civil society to function as a resource for reconciliation and democratization.

Chapter 5 delves deeper into the role of NGOs as policy advocates. The argument that NGOs can contribute to the processes of democratization are largely premised on the ability of NGOs to effect changes in government policy. Additionally, by working together NGOs are able to build networks that persuade governments to amend their policies. A detailed look at NGO–government and NGO–NGO relations reveals that there appears to be a distinct gap between the EU policy rhetoric and how these relationships play out in practice. The local interests and concerns that govern these relationships are different in the Turkish context, leading to different strategies being adopted by the actors involved.

Chapter 6 hones in on the nature of the funding environment in Turkish civil society. This chapter investigates the complementarity between the EU funding framework and the opportunities and shortcomings that actually exist within Turkish civil society. It also explores the kinds of funding choices NGOs make in this context. EU funding initiatives do address important areas of NGO work, such as advocacy, where domestic funding is rarely forthcoming. However, the complicated procedures that surround EU funding have meant that NGOs react in a number of different ways when faced with the opportunity to apply for EU funding. Some of these responses clearly contest the assumptions EU policy makes about the nature of civil society and NGOs in Turkey.

The tensions between EU policy and the behaviour of Turkish NGOs are explored further in Chapter 7. This chapter looks at the unanticipated outcomes that are generated by the policy process, and identifies four NGO roles that relate to such outcomes: translators, brokers, navigators and antagonists. The rigidity of the EU's project framework generates various different strategies among NGOs that contribute to the emergence of these roles. The main finding of this chapter relates to the unpredictability of social action and the difficulties involved in setting out a programme of project activities that have particular outcomes attached to them.

Chapter 8 concludes by drawing together the main debates of the earlier chapters in order to assess the lessons that can be learnt about NGO engagement in donor-sponsored policy processes, and the ways in which democratization and Europeanization unfold.

2
Europeanization from a Civil Society Perspective

Civil society remains essentially a Western concept. Our understanding of it has been greatly influenced by the historical path civil society has taken in Western Europe and North America. What relevance, then, can it have in the context of Turkey, a country with a Muslim population and a past steeped in Islamic traditions and history? Moreover, what does it mean to speak of 'Europeanization' of civil society in this context?

In order to answer these questions, the chapter first visits the theoretical landscape of civil society through the ideas of four key thinkers who continue to influence our understanding of civil society. The purpose here is to identify parallels between the development of the idea of civil society in the West and the way civil society has become 'operationalized' in the context of civil society development programmes elsewhere. The third section of the chapter argues that the character of civil society in the Turkish context will inevitably draw on its sociocultural roots and therefore look different from its European counterparts. The fourth and final section of the chapter considers the relevance of the Europeanization debate in the context of Turkish civil society.

The chapter argues that Western conceptions of civil society do carry relevance, yet at the same time it is important to recognize the limits of how far it is possible to stretch the parallels between Western and Turkish civil society development. The purpose of this chapter is to delineate some of the central strands of thought that characterize Western civil society theory, describe how a particular concept of civil society has been applied to civil society development policy, and to consider the relevance of such an approach in the Turkish context.

The Western origins of the idea of civil society

The way 'civil society' is understood today begins its journey from the eighteenth century. Up until then the concept was regarded as coterminous with the state. Whether we look at Cicero's *societas civilis*, Aristotle's *koinonia politike* or Kant's *bürgerliche Gesellschaft*, the essence of the term indicated a process of social development to a point where society can be described as 'civilized' (Kumar, 1993, p. 377). However, through industrialization and the development of modern, more complex societies, the idea of civil society was also being modernized.

Adam Ferguson

It was at this time that state and civil society were first seen as two separate entities, as was the case in Adam Ferguson's (1723–1816) 'Essay on the History of Civil Society' in 1767. Two important points about the nature of modern civil society are raised by Ferguson (1995). First, civil society is intricately intertwined with the institutions of modern commercial economy. Ferguson in fact treats it as a by-product of modern division of labour and worries that the modern division of labour will cause a loss of public spirit. Through the division of labour, society begins to resemble a complex machine where each individual has an increasingly specialized role. In this context, individuals become detached from the communal spirit, and public spiritedness is replaced with self-serving goals and by greed and avarice, leading to the corruption of societal values. Personal advancement becomes a priority, superseding the concern for others as well as for public spirit. Therefore, Ferguson claims that 'the separation of professions, while it seems to promise improvement of skill [...] serves, in some measure, to break the bands of society' (1995, p. 12). As these bands are broken and communal interests wither away, the subsequent corruption of public life paves the way for political despotism. The evolution of modern civil society, given its strong association with modern commercial relations can easily lead to public disregard for anything but self-interest, and thus prepare the ground for a despotic state to emerge.

Second, Ferguson argues that civil society can protect modern society from such negative social consequences. As much as we are selfish, we are also highly social animals and flourish by maintaining active social relations that 'incline us to live with our fellow-creatures, and to do them good' (1995, p. 51). We are not governed by our selfish interests alone, but also depend on a more complex set of social interactions based on the ethical and moral values that bind us to a particular community. Ferguson calls for these social values to play a larger part in the conduct of our lives and in this way curb the negative side effects of the division of labour.

Georg Hegel

Hegel's (1770–1831) work on civil society connects with Ferguson in its effort to reconcile the tension between private and public interests. Perhaps most notably, his writings took a significant stride towards consolidating the idea of civil society as an entity separate from the state. Following in the footsteps of the Scottish enlightenment, Hegel applied the pioneering idea of a market that was independent of the state and treated the behaviour of individuals outside the market in a similar fashion. Civil society, for Hegel, was thus a 'set of social practices which are constituted by the logic of the market' (Chandhoke, 1995, p. 117). Consequently, Hegel argued that individuals' particular needs and wants govern their behaviour in civil society. This was the first principle of civil society he put forward (Hegel, 1952, §182). Self-seeking individuals aiming to fulfil their private needs are the building blocks of civil society. However, if our primary instinct is to have our own needs fulfilled, with complete disregard for the needs of others, our society would not survive: 'Particularity by itself [...] destroys itself' (Hegel, 1952, §185). The second principle – universality – represents the conventions and customs of a given society that form constraints on what is regarded as acceptable behaviour and which aim to mediate this destructive tendency. This is how the innate tendency of civil society to pursue self-seeking ends is being kept in check – through the interplay between particular and universal.

> [In] the course of the actual attainment of selfish ends – an attainment conditioned in this way by universality – there is formed a system of complete interdependence, wherein the livelihood,

happiness, and legal status of one man is interwoven with the livelihood, happiness, and rights of all.

Hegel (1952, §183)

Despite the clear similarities in their assessments, Hegel appears more cynical than Ferguson. He does not believe that people are innately public-spirited, rather that we are coaxed to cooperate because this ensures that a broader set of our needs and interests will be met. There is a constant ebb and flow being played out between the particular/individual and the universal/public interests that needs somehow to be controlled. The state constitutes the highest form of ethical life, which is why, for Hegel, public authorities are ultimately responsible for ensuring that universal needs are not overshadowed by the particular, self-seeking demands of individuals (Hegel, 1952, §188). In this sense Hegel considers these state institutions as civil society because their primary role is to regulate the exchanges that take place within civil society (Chandhoke, 1995, p. 126). By enforcing a set of laws, the administration of justice and the police can ensure that each person's right to property is respected and recognized. This helps to mediate each individual's innate predisposition to seek others' property.

Alexis de Tocqueville

While Hegel emphasized the separation of civil society from the state, Alexis de Tocqueville (1805–1859) emphasized the capacity of civil society to check the excesses of state power and in so doing offer a counterbalance to the state. In this sense civil society is also seen as a key ingredient of democracy. De Tocqueville's book *Democracy in America*, published in 1832, makes a persuasive case for civil society as a bulwark against despotism (1998). In so doing, de Tocqueville develops further the separation of state and civil society proposed by Hegel. He argues that high levels of associationalism provide citizens with a way to resist the power of the state and thus protect the democratic majority from the whims of the ruling minority.

De Tocqueville was particularly concerned with the consequences of equality of conditions (in terms of income), which he believed to increase the threat of despotism. As the equality of social conditions becomes increasingly prevalent, the citizens will also become less dependent on the support of their community. They will be able to reach satisfactory educational standards and acquire sufficient material possessions to satisfy their own needs. Such citizens will have a reduced interest in the affairs of the community, becoming socially less active and withdrawing from a role in the administration of local affairs (de Tocqueville, 1998, p. 206). The emerging gap in local administration will be filled by the central government. Over time the accumulation of power in the hands of the central government will lead to the development of a despotic state. It was as an answer to this dilemma of a despotic state by stealth that de Tocqueville introduced the role of local associations. These should be given responsibility over local affairs, which bear relevance to the everyday welfare of the community and are thus likely to engage and interest citizens.

The enthusiasm for establishing local associations was one characteristic of the American society that struck a chord with de Tocqueville. He saw an added value in freely formed associations. These would not only protect against individualism and despotic government but also provide a way for citizens to take initiative and organize themselves around issues they felt were important. De Tocqueville noticed that it would be possible to exert considerable influence through such associations:

> As soon as several of the inhabitants of the United States have taken up an opinion or a feeling which they wish to promote in the world, they look out for mutual assistance; and as soon as they have found one another out, they combine. From that moment they are no longer isolated men, but a power seen from afar, whose actions serve for an example and whose language is listened to.
>
> De Tocqueville (1998, p. 218)

These associational activities emerge organically from the actions of citizens and serve to influence government decision-making, leading de Tocqueville to consider this kind of proactive self-organization as a sign of a civilized nation (de Tocqueville, 1998, p. 219). Associations have the ability to remedy the individualistic tendencies that the increased equality of conditions brings about. In order to protect democracy, therefore, the number of associations should increase in parallel with rising equality.

Antonio Gramsci

Although Gramsci's starting point for explaining the relationship between state and civil society is not too dissimilar from de Tocqueville's, his conclusions are starkly different. For Gramsci, however, the separation of state and civil society was not quite as clear-cut as for de Tocqueville, and thus civil society was not necessarily pictured as a counterbalance to the state. As civil society could protect society from the state, it could also be an accomplice in retaining the hegemony and power of a tyrannical state. There is no inherent relationship between the size of civil society and the health of democracy.

The motivation for Gramsci's work on civil society came largely from a desire to understand why the Communists in the 1920s and 1930s in Italy failed to execute the revolution. His conclusion was that they had made a mistake in focusing their efforts on capturing the state because this would not capture power (Jones, 2006; Simon, 1991). Instead, Gramsci argued, they should have focused on capturing people's minds and gain their consent through civil society, and thus create a counterhegemony that can challenge the hegemony of the state. In constructing his theory, Gramsci therefore saw an intricate web of relations existing between civil society and the state. The role of civil society was not, as de Tocqueville depicted, to protect society from a despotic state. It was rather the opposite: to protect the state from society. It is the interplay between civil society and political society that formed the tentacles of power in society.

According to Gramsci, civil society is neither a sphere of freedom nor a source of democracy, but instead a sphere of hegemony. This is the avenue that the ruling classes use to exert and retain their power through non-violent means. By controlling the production of ideas within civil society, the state elite with the support of the bourgeoisie is able to manufacture consent for the current state of socio-political affairs. Gramsci proposed to challenge this through a counterhegemonic struggle through civil society that would problematize the dominant ideas and offer new ideas in their stead, and by so doing capture the minds and consent of the people. Gramsci's work questions the extent to which civil society remains an enabling concept.

So what exactly is the picture of civil society that emerges from these four accounts? There are five broad observations worth noting. First, civil society emerges from the development of a modern market economy and diverse commercial society that establishes its independence from the state. Second, civil society offers a counterbalance to the state and thus forms an integral part of democracy and democratization. Third, civil society is not an inherently virtuous space where citizens engage in altruistic and cooperative behaviour. It is also a space for self-interest, competition and unequal power relations. Fourth, this means that civil society should also be seen as a site of struggle, where hegemonic and counterhegemonic scramble for dominance. Finally, in all its permutations the notion of civil society resonates strongly with social change – civil society has been described both as a consequence of change and in itself an agent of change.

Donors and civil society

Following Gramsci, the concept of civil society fell gradually into disuse both in the academic world as well as in politics. It was in the late 1980s that the East European dissident activist revitalized the concept, looking at the historical roots of civil society and refashioning these in their contemporary, counterhegemonic political discourse. This intellectual pursuit was joined by many Western academics whose contributions further fleshed out the theoretical underpinnings for a modern-day reformulation of civil society.[1] This debate remains contested and continues to be appropriated for different ideological purposes, particular by actors on the left and right of the political spectrum. By and large it has been the liberal democratic model of civil society, which emphasizes the separation of civil society from the state and the links between civil society and democratization that dominates the political, policy and academic discourses on the subject. These views are contrasted by the more critical perspectives drawing on Gramsci and contemporary anthropological perspectives that highlight civil society as a site of hegemony and struggle, or as a highly contextual site of associationalism.

The role of civil society in the context of donor policies largely follows the liberal democratic model that sees civil society as an important constituent of both democratic and economic development. The work of Robert Putnam, a neo-Tocquevillean scholar par excellence, paves the way to explaining how the economic and democratic arguments in favour of civil societal development have been made by donor institutions like the EU. While these considerations are relevant to international donor institutions all over the world, the particular narrative of civil society as a 'third sector' is highly relevant to how civil society is viewed in the context of EU enlargement policy.

Civil society and democratic development

Robert Putnam makes a persuasive case for considering civil society organizations as an integral part of democracy. CSOs have an external impact on democracy through the demands they make on government by advocating for a particular cause. Internally, within civil society this type of activity fosters 'habits of cooperation and public-spiritedness' that develop the civil skills required for participation in public life and 'inculcates democratic habits' (Putnam, 2000, p. 212). Putnam's work continues the Tocquevillean tradition of connecting a vibrant civil society with a well-functioning democracy. In this view, civil society is taken as a given good, and it is taken for granted that a civil society under the auspices of the state forms the best social and political framework available. Indeed, for international donor agencies, the three core components of democracy-building are support for free and fair elections, state institutions and civil society. Channelling support to CSOs is therefore integrally linked to these broader aims of democratization. This has aspired towards the development of an ideal type of civil society that entails not only broader citizen involvement but an ability to articulate the interests of citizens so as to hold the government accountable (Carothers, 1999, p. 86; Mitlin, 2004, p. 4).

Western donor agencies have thus actively engaged with civil society strengthening programmes in the belief that there is an integral relationship between civil society and democracy. Drawing on the conclusion of the neo-Tocquevillean school, donors felt that by offering technical and financial assistance to NGOs, it would be possible to build democracy (Ishkanian, 2008, p. 5). Civil society has been romanticized and, particularly in the American policy circles, regarded as the quintessential element of democracy promotion, a view which in the post-September 11 world has become increasingly influential (Ishkanian, 2008, p. 6). The dominance of the American view on the relationship between civil society and democracy in donor circles has led to what has been termed the

'Americanization of the debate' (Carothers, 1999; Howell and Pearce, 2001a). The role of CSOs as it is understood in the Western context and from a neo-Tocquevillean point of view has dominated the way in which donors have opted to engage in civil society development in third countries.

The case of the Middle East offers a useful example of the seamless links between economic and democratic aspirations and civil society initiatives. Both American and European efforts of promoting democracy in the Middle East have been incorporated in the broader context of the 'War on Terror' (Carothers, 2004, p. 7; Howell and Lind, 2009). Thomas Carothers has described the American donor strategy which has unfolded as threefold in nature, focusing on economic reform as well as indirect and direct democracy promotion (2004, pp. 241–7). The 'economics first' approach believes in the transformative power of economic development, where an independent and pluralist private sector will help the growth of an independent middle class. This will in turn bolster support for and independence of civil society. Indirect support for democracy in turn focuses on promoting good governance and strengthening civil society. The aim is not to tackle the deeper political issues, but to provide a framework within which the political context that prevents democratization from taking place could be resolved. Civil society strengthening here has taken the form of support for advocacy groups working on human rights, women's rights, environment and anti-corruption initiatives. These examples suggest that liberal democratic understanding of civil society forms an important part of Western donor policy.

Civil society as a third sector

In the domestic context of USA and Europe, a strong case has been made for encouraging greater civil society participation in the policymaking process and service delivery as a means to improve government effectiveness. Putnam, in his book *Making Democracy Work*, puts forth an argument that associational networks have a direct effect on government performance (Putnam, Leonardi and Nanetti, 1994). In this study of Italy's regions, identical regional governments displayed higher levels of effectiveness where civic engagement was stronger. Voter turnout, newspaper readership, membership in choral societies and football clubs were among indicators of civic engagement (Putnam, 1995; Putnam, Leonardi and Nanetti, 1994).

It is the quality of this civic community that determines the quality of democracy, Putnam argues.

In the early 1970s, Amitai Etzioni discussed his vision for a third sector in a seminal article on the subject. He argued that a third alternative had been added to the traditional debate over how to serve our needs. In addition to public and private options, the third sector could offer a new alternative (but not replace the already existing options). Thus, a 'method must be developed to combine the "best of both worlds" – efficiency and expertise from the business world with public interest, accountability and broader planning from government' (Etzioni, 1973, p. 315). In a similar fashion, Lester Salamon in the 1980s pushed welfare state theory to move beyond explanations that were limited by the 'market failure–government failure' theory. Focusing on the case of the United States, he called for a much more serious consideration of the role the voluntary sector already played in the provision of government services and how the voluntary sector was proving to be a great help in the development of government policy. Salamon termed this 'third party government' (Salamon, 1981, 1987).

It is this role envisaged for civil society today, interweaving with government policy and service delivery, that is captured by the term 'third sector'. Like civil society, the term 'third sector' is used to describe the space outside of the state and the market. It has an intermediary role between the public and private sectors, balancing the political interests of the public sector with the economic interests of the private (Anheier and Seibel, 1989, p. 9). From a policy point of view, the benefit of greater civil society – or third sector – involvement in policy implementation is in finding a happy medium between social and political integration and economic development (Anheier and Seibel, 1989, p. 10).

For example, in the United Kingdom the third way rhetoric of former Prime Minister Tony Blair and the New Labour party stems from a similar intellectual base. Anthony Giddens' book *The Third Way* (1998) is an attempt to capture the policy implications of this rhetoric and to put some theoretical flesh around the skeleton of policymaking that began to emerge. According to Giddens, the absolute faith in the free market represented by the conservative political leadership in Britain was unwise; what was needed instead was a system that combines the best of the public and private sectors. The role of the state here is to coordinate, or steer the individual and communal efforts to pursue a better quality of life. The choice that is presented to citizens is not a simple one between a state-managed economy and a free market because a multitude of intermediary agencies located in civil society (individuals, social groups, voluntary sector) are envisaged to work in partnership with public and private sectors. The role of CSOs is not viewed purely as potential service-deliverers. Civil society is believed to have a political role to play as well. This two-pronged approach is evident in the actions of the previous UK government, as on the one hand it established the "Office of the Third Sector" to explore the service-delivery potential of civil society. At the same time the government devised a policy on 'Community Partnerships' that aimed to give greater decision-making powers to local civil society groups over issues concerning local communities (Communities and Local Government, 2008). Civil society, therefore, has both a policy role and a political role to play. The ideas that inform third-way thinking have also had an important impact on the approach the EU together with other European governments take in their relationship with civil society.

The underlying tendency is to view civil society as always making a positive contribution; the more groups there are the better. The way in which donors conceive of civil society either as contributing towards policy effectiveness or democratization has meant that often only a narrow band of NGOs registers on the donors' radar. This approach ignores not only the diversity of organizations in civil society but also the myriad of other motivations for CSOs to do their work. These organizations can represent different political ideologies and struggle against each other as well as against the state. The donor approach will create winners and losers among the local CSOs and bring up new sources of contention and competition, particularly where the culture represented by the donor agencies is strikingly different. The next two sections consider further the importance of context, where the discussion shifts to reflect on the challenges that the Turkish case presents in light of the theoretical positions on civil society presented thus far.

Muslim civil society

> Islam is the blueprint of a social order. It holds that a set of rules exist, external, divinely ordained, and independent of the will of men, which defines the proper ordering of society.
>
> Gellner (1981, p. 1)

These opening lines of Ernest Gellner's *Muslim Society* allude to what is at the core of the debate over the existence of Muslim civil society. Gellner argues that in Islam both the civil and the political are governed by religious tenets leaving no room for individuality to flourish. Christianity, in contrast, relinquished aspirations for political power from the outset, and in particular since the Protestant Reformation (1517–79) and the gradual secularization of European societies that followed. The separation of religion and politics in this way has significantly contributed to the emergence of the secular state in the Christian world. This is much more difficult to achieve in Islam because religious law remains the guiding principle for both politics and society. The *umma*, the overarching community of all Muslims, prevails over the individual. The focus remains on group rights, not on individual rights (Kazemi, 2002, p. 232).

The benefits of the existence of these individual structures in society are spelled out in more detail by Gellner's idea of a 'modular man'. According to Gellner, a modular man is one who

> can combine into specific-purpose, *ad hoc*, limited associations, without binding himself by some blood ritual. He can leave an association when he comes to disagree with its policy without being open to the charge of treason. [...] *This* is civil society: the forging of links which are effective even though they are flexible, specific, instrumental.
>
> Gellner (1994, p. 42)

The conditions within a Muslim society make the emergence of a modular man unlikely. Islam, argues Gellner, favours the traditional communal bonds at the expense of fostering the individualism of a modular man. Instead of opting for moving along with modernity and becoming modular, the tendency in Muslim countries has been to remain communalist and resist bonds that exist outside kinship and religion. This kind of associationalism lacks the 'flexibility, specificity and instrumentality' that emerge in a modern, secular and pluralist civil society (Gellner, 1995, pp. 98–102).

Şerif Mardin, a Turkish scholar, also argues that Muslim countries are inherently different, making emergence of civil society unlikely. He has famously described civil society as a 'Western dream, a historical aspiration', which has become focused on human agency, on the 'ability to dream the dream' (Mardin, 1995, p. 278). The

Muslim dream, on the other hand aspired for a 'social equilibrium created under the aegis of a just prince' (Mardin, 1995, p. 285). This is the crucial difference Mardin sees between the East and the West. While the notion of civility – the ethical (how individuals should behave) and moral (notions of right and wrong) tenets – translates into Islamic terms, civil society with its inferences to individualism, agency and freedom does not. Although Muslim states are gradually modernizing and acquiring Western institutional characteristics, the dream remains different. It remains the business of the state to ensure that citizens adhere to the moral and ethical teachings of Islam (Moussali, 1994).

The placement of moral and ethical values within the realm of government is possibly the most important characteristic of Islam that makes many regard it unable to accommodate democracy. The liberal democratic point of view would not allow for the government to impose a particular set of values (moral, religious) upon its citizens because this would infringe on their rights as individuals. Hegel, agreeing with the liberal democratic perspective, saw the state as a source of neutral rationality that enabled it to arbitrate between different particular interests in society. Gramsci in contrast pointed to the façade of democracy and neutrality that the capitalist state was able to maintain with the support of civil society. Is it, therefore, possible to say that an approach to governance and political life that emphasizes liberal individualistic values is universally applicable? On one side of the debate lies an argument that criticizes liberal individualism for its degenerative impact on social solidarity and for its lack of relevance in societies where social identity is derived from a particular cultural or communal source. It would be more appropriate, therefore, to see individuals as embedded in particular communities recognize differences and support the interdependence of groups (Sandel, 1996; Young, 1993). On the other side of the debate we find an argument that criticizes Islam for its tendency to smother individualism, for prioritizing group rights at the expense of individual rights. Because of this, Muslim societies are deemed unable to sustain a genuine civil society or democracy.

Muslim civil society as 'society with ethics'

Perhaps the most elaborate and substantial critique of the universal claims behind the liberal democratic perspective comes from within the communitarian movement of political thought. It offers an alternative framework which places emphasis on local communal values, making the argument that ethical and moral beliefs found in a particular context must be the bases of any functioning political system (Etzioni, 1973; Sandel, 1996; Walzer, 1983). Although the communitarian movement makes no specific reference to Islam, scholars exploring the nature of civil society in the Muslim world have found much common ground in these ideas.

The members of the communitarian movement have been critical of the liberal point of view, aiming their arrows at the impact liberal individualism is having on social solidarity and active citizenship. Their concern is with the lack of traditional moral values, which ought to form the backbone of any vibrant civil society (Rawls, 1972; Sandel, 1996), critiquing the emphasis placed on economics and free market individualism by others (Hayek, 1960; Nozick, 1974). In response, there is a call for heightened values of social trust and community building in order to rebuild social solidarity in Western societies (Sajoo, 2004, pp. 218–9).

As Iris Marion Young has argued, the ideal of liberal individualism tends to promote an assimilationist model that is unlikely to reflect people's experiences. Liberal individualism challenges the notion of difference that arises from group identity, and any discrimination that is based on group privileges. Therefore, according to liberal individualism, citizens should be viewed only as individuals, not as members of groups (Young, 1993). The trouble with such interpretation, observes Young, is that it ignores other more legitimate reasons for preserving group identities. As long as groups are not linked to oppression or exclusion of other groups, group identity can be an important element of how individual identity becomes embedded in the broader society. It is more sensible to consider individuals as part of a particular social context, defined by the community within which they live. Interdependence between groups is the means through which it is possible to create social cohesion, argues Young.

The role of ethical and moral beliefs in society is a critical point of contention between the liberal view on civil society and an Islamic interpretation (Sajoo, 2004). The liberal view wishes to push any role for moral and ethical concerns strictly to the private sphere. This position is based on a conviction that any restrictions on citizens' freedom should be premised on upholding negative liberty (the absence of constraints that limit individual's range of possible actions) and in so doing augment the plurality of goals that citizens are able to pursue. This stands in stark contrast to the role ethics and morals play in an Islamic public sphere. Ethics and morality should bear upon the types of goals that citizens and communities wish to pursue. The principles of social ethics ought to be discussed in and by civil society. Barricading these away from the public sphere would contradict an Islamic worldview.

Society with an ethical compass is seen as broadly beneficial in the Muslim context, particularly where properly functioning democratic institutions are lacking. In the absence of democracy, the incivility that may follow is ameliorated by the existence of ethical tenets that govern individuals' conduct in the public. For Sajoo, the content of such tenets does not have to differ between Islam and the West. The principles of 'social solidarity, self-help and integrity' are recognized social values in both secular and Muslim public domains (2004, p. 234). Kamali has also pointed to the importance of social solidarity as a key condition for civil society to exist, arguing that it is not possible to reduce the theory of civil society to a simple political relationship between the people and state. Social solidarity offers a sense of belonging to a society (2001 p. 460). Seen this way, civil society in the Muslim context can offer the means to establish tenets of ethical life that are relevant to that context, and at the same time have many commonalities with Western values.

Others take a more simplified approach, arguing that there is nothing particularly special about the Muslim world. It operates much like the West, but with a time lag. Many of the Muslim countries are only now in the throes of modernization, adapting to the modern socio-economic formations that are taking shape. This process will create its own CSOs that will push for participatory forms of governance (Ibrahim, 1998, p. 30). Through the process of modernization and industrialization Ibrahim identifies four factors that have contributed to the growth of civil society: growing unmet needs, growth in educated citizenry, growing individual financial resources and increased margins of freedom (Ibrahim, 1998, pp. 39–40). Ibrahim adopts a similar approach as Ferguson and Hegel have, taking the commercial and social changes instigated by industrialization as the starting point. Under these conditions CSOs are very likely to emerge, facing one of two possible outcomes. The autocratic regimes and Islamic activists may try to squeeze civil society out of the public arena altogether. Alternatively, the regime and the religious activists may attempt to appropriate or win over civil society to their own cause (Ibrahim, 1998, p. 51). It is this last scenario that, for Ibrahim, holds the greatest promise for civil societal development because it contains at least as much promise for further democratic development as there is against it.

Consequences of modernization are often beyond the control of states and offer an example of how social and economic change can lead to various outcomes that question the uncompromising nature of Islamic political philosophy. Under the waves of modernization, many choose to escape rural poverty, leave their traditional bonds of kinship and tribal loyalties behind, and move into cities, often congregating in shanty towns. In Iran, Islamist groups have given a voice to shanty dwellers and mobilized them in their cause (Kamali, 2001, p. 471). Although in this case the activism that emerged reinforced existing religious social norms, it offers evidence of the new windows of opportunity that modernization creates for mobilizing social forces in civil societal activity. Another consequence of modernization is the emergence of the 'moderate fundamentalist', an Islamic activist with a vision to compromise. The moderate fundamentalist is open to dialogue, compromise and to the values of universal rights, freedom and civil society. The call for social justice found in a religious society is replaced by a demand for pluralism and tolerance of difference (Moussali, 1994, p. 118). These kinds of developments question the immutability of Muslim society suggested by Gellner, and argue against treating Muslim societies as one homogenous group. There is much variation between Muslim societies across country contexts, an example of which is the different paths taken towards modernization and economic development.

Can civil society exist in a Muslim context? There is no simple answer to this question, but it seems that those arguing on the opposite sides take a different view on what civil society means. Islam is not only a religion but also a political theory that provides the legitimate basis of political power. Thus, it is not possible to locate Islam purely in the public realm, for it will also remain an energetic political force. The Western tradition of treating state and civil society as entirely separate, antagonistic entities does not seem appropriate. If this structural separation is at the heart of what is meant by civil society, then it will be more difficult to accept the existence of civil society in the Muslim context. However, if the search for civil society is focused on the values and modes of behaviour that civil society upholds – civility, social solidarity, social justice and public ethics as well as morals – then we may well conclude that there are good grounds for civil society to exist in the Muslim context. The rise of Fascism in the West, for example, showed that the existence of a public space independent of the state is in itself no guarantee of democracy and tolerance. The nature of the values that civil society chooses to uphold is an equally important part of the equation for democracy. To this end, there are no reasons set in stone as to why Muslim societies could not open up to the values that support and encourage associationalism along lines that are both pluralist and tolerant.

These observations correspond awkwardly with the donor policies aiming at democratization through civil society funding. It may be unhelpful, even counterproductive to promote external funding as developing civil society as a counterpoint to the state, when there is still a much stronger link between the two. The liberal individualistic logic that informs such policy is likely to gain less traction in a society where strong cultural group affinities continue to define individual identities as embedded in particular communities.

The relevance of civil society debates in the Turkish context

The case of Turkey weaves together the various strands of the previous debate.[2] The donor ideas about civil society remain highly relevant because they explain how civil society is understood in the European context, a context to which Turkey is intricately connected to by the EU pre-accession process. At the same time the debates on Muslim civil society resonate strongly with the secularization debates in Turkey that concern the role of religion in Turkish society. The juxtaposition of these various political and cultural elements leaves Turkey outside the ideal types on either side. Given the unique context of Turkey, it is then important to consider the likely impact of EU civil society policy grounded in a third sector approach and in liberal democratic ideals about how civil society is expected to contribute to the Europeanization and democratization processes in Turkey.

Through its application for EU membership, Turkey has made its Western aspirations clear, and Western understanding of civil society is a relevant part of this commitment. The Turkish republic was founded in 1923 on a series of Westernizing reforms that have become a defining feature of its character. Creating a modern Turkish state from the ashes of the Ottoman Empire involved a break with the past, at least in terms of rhetoric. However, Turkish society had already been gripped by the question of how to synthesize Western and Eastern values in the Ottoman/Turkish melting pot (Parla, 1985). These attempts at synthesis have in part taken place in civil society, and in so doing left their imprint on the character of Turkish civil society today. The values of a modern Western civilization that were adopted were imposed from above – as Kadioğlu poignantly describes it, the question was not one of 'who are the Turks', but rather 'who are the Turks going to be' (1996, p. 177).

We return for a moment to Hegel's idea of the interplay between the particular and universal, where the particular needs of individuals govern their actions, to be limited only by the rules that govern universality. In Turkey's case, the particular view of the reformers expanded into a new definition of universality that was based on a Turkish nationalist–republican vision of modernity (Seufert, 2000). What was going to be regarded as appropriate behaviour in society was reinterpreted on the basis of the modernizers' agenda, and the public authorities became the defenders of a particular interpretation of what was meant by universal. The function of civil society, to evoke a Gramscian image, was to dig the protective trenches around the state and to ensure the hegemony of the ideology of the elite. As the processes of state-building that preceded this did not resolve the underlying and competing private needs, the reforms merely brushed away a fire that, out of sight, continued to smoulder. As such, the adoption of Western values was selective and limited, and for decades civil society was smothered by the republican assimilationist ideas of Turkishness, allowed only to flourish in support of the state.

Gradually from the early 1980s onwards a much broader array of civil societal actors was allowed increasing scope to operate. In the aftermath of the 1980 military coup, the military leadership looked to Islamic organizations in particular as potential allies in ensuring that support for Marxist and Fascist movements responsible for the significant social unrest that had led to the coup was going to be contained in the future. Islamic groups, the green movement and the women's movement all began to gain greater freedom to operate. However, through these developments the smouldering, competing sets of interests that had been contained by a strong state saw the light of day. The groups representing these competing points of view found it difficult to tolerate each other and engage in a rational debate (Keyman, 1995). What has emerged from the increasingly autonomous civil society does not, therefore, resonate well with the Tocquevillean reflection of civil society as a counterpoint of despotism. The various organizations are in competition with each other, and the nature of this competition is more a reflection of the Gramscian hegemonic versus counterhegemonic struggles. The lack of tolerance can be at least partly explained by the unresolved nature of important social debates, such as the terms under which secularism and Islam can comfortably coexist in Turkey.

A key development in all of this has been the rise of the Islamic dimension of Turkish society since 1980 (Yavuz, 2009). The normative, Western view of what makes civil society is based on the Western experience of modernization and nation-building, and this does not comfortably align with the realities of a Muslim society. The neoliberal values not only clash with the values of a Muslim society but also with the values of a communitarian understanding of the Western society that prioritizes social solidarity and active citizenship. The arguments that challenge the existence of Muslim civil society are based on a neoliberal understanding of civil society, and the universal relevance of this approach is contested both by the Turkish context and the communitarian point of view. By widening the scope of our understanding of civil society to include concepts such as social trust, social solidarity and community building, it is possible to begin to see significant overlaps between Islamic and Western values. Both consist of individuals that join together as members of a society upholding certain universal ethical standards. The case of Turkey, a secular country with a Muslim population, therefore, cuts straight to the heart of this debate surrounding the cultural relativity of civil society. This also raises important and interesting questions about what the Europeanization of Turkish civil society will mean in practice.

In reflecting on the usefulness of civil society as a concept in non-Western contexts, the distinctions drawn by David Lewis offer a helpful starting point (2001a). First, there are many who advocate for a Western understanding of civil society to be universally accepted as the only idea of civil society that there is. This view is difficult to dismiss and will always remain relevant, if for no other reason than for the economic power behind donor funding of civil society initiatives. The second point of view argues that civil society originates from a particular political and cultural pathway traversed in Europe, and has little meaning outside countries immediately related to this context. The third view takes an adaptive approach, arguing that civil society does remain relevant, but it takes on different local meanings and it is therefore unhelpful if we try to conceptualize it too rigidly. Finally, Lewis offers the view that the whole question is 'a wrong one to ask'; whether or not officially recognized, civil society has in fact been implicated in the local history of non-Western contexts for a long time. The relevance of civil society as a concept in a non-Western context is likely to hinge not on one, but on all four viewpoints. For example, in Turkey, the impact of a universal conception through donor funding and EU involvement is undeniable. Yet, it seems likely that aspects of the European understanding of civil society as a third sector bear less relevance to the case of present-day Turkey, and similarly there are aspects to Turkish civil society that exist only in that context. These different viewpoints remind us to push for a multidimensional understanding. In so doing, it suggests a strategy for how to understand the existence of civil society in non-Western contexts – as a hybrid where both domestic and external influences conflate in a new, locally relevant variant. The aim here is to explore how a particular hybrid that has been influenced by the EU accession context comes to being in Turkey.

It is therefore important to study how civil society gets translated in different political and cultural contexts. The dominant, universal notions of what civil society means are undoubtedly exported by donor practices, but exactly what kind of social and political impact this will have is undetermined. The usefulness of civil society as a concept depends less on abstract definitions than on ensuring that ideas are grounded in actual experiences (Glasius, Lewis and Seckinelgin, 2004). Particular cultural ideas interact with the reputed universal relevance of civil society and influence how the concept is 'manifested in practice, in everyday social behaviour' (Hann and Dunn, 1996).

Europeanization in non-Western contexts

What does it mean to speak of Europeanization in non-Western contexts? Can it amount to more than a technical and bureaucratic process of policy harmonization? In what way is civil society, seen here as an inherently socio-political construct (rather than as a mere technical instrument for policy delivery) affected by such a policy process? Recognizing the importance of understanding the impact of local context and the agency of local actors, and merging this with existing approaches to studying European integration, the approach here takes 'sociological institutionalism' as its starting point. This approach draws attention to the importance of actors' subjective values that draw on sources such as norms, identity and culture (Eilstrup-Sangiovanni, 2006, p. 395). Such an approach is particularly relevant to the study of NGOs, as common values are an important bonding agent between organizational actors. The decisions NGOs make in terms of organizational change, for example, are not necessarily utility-maximizing, rational calculations based on effectiveness. Instead, such decisions are reflective of broader questions. Hall and Taylor, for instance, argue that organizational change comes about when it 'enhances the social legitimacy of the organization or its participants' (1996, p. 949). In this way organizations are deeply embedded in their social context. The way for us to explain policy outcomes is therefore contingent on the informal rules and norms that shape the interests of actors involved. A central piece of the puzzle, then, is the socialization of EU policy: how the local actors internalize the EU rules and norms, and how the outcomes of this process in turn influence actors' self-perceptions and interests (Eilstrup-Sangiovanni, 2006, p. 395). The lens of sociological institutionalism therefore opens EU policy and any related Europeanization processes to an analysis that is more sensitive of the local context. This makes it a useful conceptual tool for understanding the interaction between donor policy and NGOs.

Sociological institutionalism has received some pertinent criticism from the more sociologically attuned observers. In EU studies, rational choice theories and sociological theories of institutionalism have been artificially kept apart by attaching strategic interests to the former and normative behaviour to the latter. Insistence on this distinction is less likely to correspond with reality, for 'rational and normative behaviour are two sides of the same coin: rationality is socially constructed in the same way that norms have to be strategically deployed' (Jenson and Merand, 2010, p. 84).

In order to address the interaction between norms and strategies, the argument of the book draws on actor-oriented perspectives by way of emphasizing the scope for strategic action by local actors. The actor-oriented approach takes the diversity and heterogeneity of possible actions as its starting point. It takes particular interest in situations where there exist 'discrepancies of social interest [and] cultural interpretation' and is concerned with how these differences are mediated or transformed (Long, 2001, p. 49). This is a useful consideration in the context of Turkey's Europeanization process, as it offers insights to how such process may be negotiated by local actors. As such, actor-oriented methods form an approach that highlights the relevance of local cultural norms, together with an appreciation of the ability of local actors to make strategic decisions. It offers an insight into the messy and uncontrollable processes of socialization that take place among Turkish NGOs in terms of internalizing the rules and norms introduced by EU civil society policy.

Conclusion

The debate over whether civil society can exist in a Muslim context illustrates the multidimensionality of the concept of civil society. Thus, any application of civil society theory that pushes beyond the geographical boundaries of the West should remain sensitive to the diversity of ways in which civil society action may manifest itself and it is important to move beyond the categories of civil society action that are drawn purely from the Western/European experience.

This chapter has anchored the discussion of civil society to the ideas that emerged during the social transformations of the eighteenth and nineteenth centuries, and to the centrality of a particular Western experience of industrialization and modernization to the development of theories about civil society. Ferguson, Hegel and de Tocqueville are all examples of theorists whose work addressed the social changes that were brought about by rapid economic development. Their work highlighted the impact of the market and division of labour on the emergence of civil society, and also showed civil society as something which could ameliorate the negative side effects of economic development. De Tocqueville also argued that in the United States the impact of civil society reached beyond the social order and to the realm of political order by helping to hold the state accountable to its citizens. These thoughts continue to shine through the European and donor understandings of what is meant by civil society.

It is the apparent efficacy of civil society in bringing about economic and democratic development that makes policies aimed at advancement of civil society so attractive for policymakers. Thus, at least in terms of policy rhetoric, the contribution of civil society is viewed in wholly positive terms – the participation of civil society actors adds something positive to the existing policies and improves them. Such assumptions should be further problematized because it is questionable that such a view is wholly relevant to the Turkish case. A more contextually sensitive treatment of civil society may well be more appropriate in contexts that extend beyond the Western experience that informs the current policy debate. Furthermore, such treatment of the concept pays attention to the gap that exists between how donors understand civil society to manifest itself and what actually happens in contexts that are detached from donor reality. By drawing on sociological institutionalism and actor-oriented perspectives, the argument here suggests that where such gaps exist between policy and reality, local actors are the key to understanding how the various interests are negotiated. What such a viewpoint highlights in the case of Turkey's Europeanization is the potential gaps between the EU policy framework and reality on the ground, and how – as a consequence of this – the values and norms introduced by the EU policy framework become internalized in a particular way at the local level. To the extent that Turkish civil society is being Europeanized, this Europeanization process is likely to unfold in an uncertain and unpredictable way.

3
EU Civil Society Policy

This chapter outlines the broader context in which the EU policy towards Turkish civil society has been incubated and makes two observations about the motives behind this policy. First, NGOs serve as an *instrument* to the overall cause. They help to fill the gap between an aspirational goal of Europeanization and the current state of affairs. Second, the vision that the EU has of civil society is based on a *universal* idea of the concept. The notion of civil society, as understood in the European context, is assumed to be readily transferable to contexts that are culturally and historically different. To what extent, then, has EU civil society policy been tailored to fit the Turkish reality? The first part of this chapter provides a framework for understanding the formulation of policy and highlights the significance of policy language. The second part offers an overview of the main contours of EU civil society policy, as it has developed within the EU. The third section traces the characteristics of EU Mediterranean policy, and compares the EU approach within and outside its borders. The final section looks at EU civil society policy in Turkey, identifies two policy streams (democratization and dialogue) and draws conclusions about the nature of this policy. The assessment demonstrates the 'universality of instrumentality' by showing how civil society, in different contexts, is seen to shape into a similar instrument of change and reform, and questions the appropriateness of this strategy, given the reality of civil society activity in the Turkish context.

Approaches to understanding EU policy

Recent EU policy towards Turkey has been largely dictated by the requirements of the enlargement process. That is to say, the EU–Turkey relationship has been dominated by the unidirectional adaptation of EU policy in order for Turkey to comply with the EU *acquis* (Diez, Agnantopoulos and Kaliber, 2005). Although this is an inevitable part of the accession process, and the content of what Turkey has to adapt in terms of policy cannot be compromised, it remains important to inquire how this process operates. The nature of the process affects how individuals view the prospect of accession and determines what kind of inter-subjective meaning gets attached to the idea of EU membership (Risse-Kappen, 2001). In other words, what kind of 'societal Europeanization' takes place (Diez, Agnantopoulos and Kaliber, 2005, pp. 5–6)? How are meanings of Europeanization internalized and made meaningful to local actors?

The three forms of 'New Institutionalism' offer a useful framework conceptualizing the processes. Rational choice institutionalism supposes that actors' behaviour is driven by a 'strategic calculus' (Hall and Taylor, 1996, p. 945). With a focus on formal institutions and the actions of member states, this strand of thinking suggests that individual actors form their preferences through a process of rational calculation. Another angle to rational choice institutionalism examines the agenda-setting power as a source of influence (Eilstrup-Sangiovanni, 2006, p. 195). For example, when investigating the effectiveness of EU conditionality, Schimmelfennig and Sedelmeier found that when comparing the effectiveness of the two types of conditionality applied by the EU – democratic conditionality and *acquis* conditionality – the latter was more effective in bringing about change (2008). The political costs of adopting democratic and human rights norms as a result of EU conditionality were too high for incumbent governments. Highly nationalistic governments in particular remained resistant to the EU efforts to initiate democratic reform. It was also of relevance that *acquis* conditionality enters onstage once formal accession negotiations have begun. Thus, for Schimmelfennig and Sedelmeier the key explanatory variables were the domestic costs for governments that came with adopting EU rules, and the credibility of the promises of eventual EU accession that surround the conditionalities (Schimmelfennig and Sedelmeier, 2008; cf. Schimmelfennig, 2008; Schimmelfennig and Sedelmeier, 2004).

Historical institutionalism, on the other hand, can be seen to build on the rational choice approach by adding a temporal dimension to the analysis. Therefore, how actors behave is determined partly by the rational choices they make, yet these are conditioned by past decisions (Hall and Taylor, 1996, pp. 937–8; Kazamias and Featherstone, 2001). The historical context creates certain path dependencies that make certain actions more likely in one country and less likely in another. In this sense, the various policy documents reviewed in this chapter are dependent on the existing policy documents, forming a chain of decisions each influencing the range of possible actions available to the EU going forward. Historical institutionalism can help explain how and why certain policy trajectories have developed as policy is built on top of already existing policy. As such, these two conceptual lenses help explain how EU policy on civil society has come to take its current shape. It is against this backdrop that the role of local actors will be considered in detail in the chapters that follow.

When we discuss Europeanization in the Turkish context, the following conceptual map of the different meanings attached to the concept is useful. Diez, Agnantopoulos and Kaliber break Europeanization down to its policy, political, societal and discursive elements (2005). *Policy Europeanization* refers to the impact of European integration on policymaking, focusing primarily on the 'goodness of fit' between what is required by the next step of integration and what already exists within the country in question, followed by domestic adjustments where appropriate (Risse, Cowles and Caporaso, 2001). *Political Europeanization* focuses on the impact of European integration on political institutions and on their ability to deliver the reforms requested. In addition, this field of study concerns itself with the impact of European integration on a variety of political actors, such as political parties and interest groups. Different political agents are affected in different ways, as each agent may be hindered or empowered by certain consequences of the integration process. *Societal Europeanization*, on the other hand, focuses on questions of how social norms and identity formation may be pegged onto perceptions of European integration. Finally, *discursive Europeanization* pertains to the study of how public discourses reference the EU – whether, and to what extent, the language of 'Europe' enters the domestic public discourse.

The policy process can be approached as rational and objective. In such a case, policy is regarded as an instrument employed to pursue a predefined end result. Such policy is generally paired with an assumption that it is based on objective criteria that apply equally; it has an air of universality (Dryzek, 1990). Policy is seen as a technical, controlled exercise. On the other hand, it is also possible to see policy as an inherently political activity where various interests are constantly entering the process, and it is the outcome of a constantly evolving bargaining process (Gordon, Lewis and Young, 1977). Although policy as a rational, technical process has been widely critiqued for depoliticizing a naturally political process (Ferguson, 1990) and for placing emphasis on the institutions instead of the individual actors involved (Long, 2001), such approaches remain largely favoured among policymakers.[1]

In the 1980s the tendency to gravitate towards the rational approach to policymaking was reinforced by the increasing prevalence of 'New Public Management' (NPM) as the dominant mode of policymaking (Hood, 1995). The term encapsulates the shift that took place in how Western societies perceived the welfare state. The state and public sector were deemed to lack the efficiency required in the post-industrial era. The diversification of economic production in the face of reduced industrial output meant that a one-size-fits-all welfare state was no longer adequate. Among the changes brought about by the NPM approach were a reduced public sector role in delivering public services, competitive contracting out of public services to civil society and private sector, and an emphasis on measurable outcomes that can be used to assess performance (Hood, 1991, 1995; Ferlie, McLaughlin and Osborne, 2001). The introduction of certain private sector logic to public sector affairs thus aided the popularity of rational approaches to policymaking. Civil society was incorporated in the broader strategies for policymaking and policy implementation that stemmed from NPM. The idea of civil society as third sector, as an alternative provider of public services, had already begun to take shape in the 1970s (Etzioni, 1973). This sectoral conceptualization divides society into the sectors of state, market and the charitable sector. In this logic, the meaning of civil society is understood through the categories of state and market. The third sector, therefore, is taken to refer to the realm of professional non-profit organizations that are able to interact both with state and market actors (Richter, 2002).

The role of policy language

As the sections that follow are focused on the content of policy, it is important to highlight the language of civil society as it manifests itself in the EU policy documents. The language of these documents provide the starting point for a process which shapes the way in which local actors conceive of civil society and the way EU bureaucrats on the ground approach local civil societies. This transformative process is possible due to the power relation between the EU as a donor and the NGO as a recipient of donor funds. Civil society-related projects may shape what local civil society actors perceive as being appropriate behaviour.

The language of civil society has been described as a proxy for a particular understanding of Western political values (Seckinelgin, 2002). Seckinelgin argues that the language of civil society found in policy documents acts as a 'metaphor for western liberalism'. This metaphor is a tool that 'maps an experience from a source domain to some target domain' (e.g. from Western domain to a non-Western domain). A speaker selects a metaphor because it satisfactorily maps the experience of a new culture onto an already existing cultural understanding. Metaphor, therefore, is an 'intuition' that enables the combination of two dissimilar experiences together (Seckinelgin, 2002, pp. 357–60). The metaphor does not make the assumptions (the source domain), on which it is based, explicit. A particular understanding of civil society takes on the cloak of universality, justifies its use and protects it from further questions regarding its applicability. Understanding the approaches of international donor agencies in terms of a metaphor therefore allows us to problematize the universal usage of the civil society rhetoric (Seckinelgin, 2002, p. 361).

Policy language is deemed transformative, for it imports a set of external rules that shape people's understanding of the role they are to play. Policy language is able to differentiate people into groups of deserving and undeserving, and it is the deserving that are much more likely to engage in the desired behaviour (Crowley, Watson and Waller, 2008). The benefits of such engagement – largely financial in the case of EU project funding in Turkey – are likely to strengthen the role of such behaviour in the local context, making it an increasingly hegemonic practice. Ultimately it is the unequal power relation between the policymakers and policy recipients that gives policy language a potentially transformative effect. For example, by providing a particular content to civil society (i.e. NGOs), the policy language is likely to block out that which does not fit, even where the discarded may be a part of the local reality of civil society (Seckinelgin, 2008).

When we conceive of donor assistance for civil society not merely as a technical process of delivering aid but also as a way of exporting a set of socio-political processes and structures from Western to non-Western contexts, the implications of such policy become much more far-reaching. Donors, such as the EU, are much more likely to work with organizations that understand the metaphor – professional advocacy groups staffed with foreign-educated employees, based in the capital city (Maina, 1998). This exploration of how policy language has the potential to play out serves as an avenue for understanding the kinds of pitfalls a bureaucratic and technical approach to policy can have. This is particularly relevant in cases where policy frameworks cross cultural contexts. Ironically this is also the time when policy blueprints are often utilized. The previous section has provided a background to the origin and nature of these blueprints, as well as clarified the role policy language plays. The remainder of this chapter unravels the language of the blueprints that are utilized in EU policy formulation.

EU policy towards civil society, 1992–2003

In this section four EU policy documents from 1992 to 2003 concerning EU civil society policy are analysed. These dates are not arbitrary. The year 1992 marked the ratification of the Maastricht Treaty, which led to an increasingly critical debate on the democratic deficit that existed within the EU and the potential role of civil society in remedying this deficiency. By 2003 the policy discussions on the role of civil society had shifted away from a domestic debate to the realm of enlargement, and the document trace is picked up from here in the following sections. The overall focus is on capturing the meaning of civil society reflected in these documents as well as the justifications given for further engagement with civil society at the European level.

The documents reviewed in this chapter have been selected to illustrate the gradual evolution of EU policy on civil society since 1992. The discussion therefore focuses on a particular set of documents that help to illustrate the developing complexity of EU policy on civil society, with later sections focusing on the cases of the Mediterranean and Turkey. The documents are not therefore representative of the total range available, but rather serve as an illustration of the nature of the approach the EU opted for within each evolutionary phase. The story told by these documents not only clarifies the origins of EU civil society policy, but also explains how certain themes have become prevalent within the EU civil society discourse. The policy documents push forward two distinct roles for civil society. CSOs make a contribution to government policy either by delivering services that governments would provide otherwise, or by contributing to the decision-making process as policy is being devised. The state–civil society partnership is thus reinforcing a particular vision of state–civil society relations.

In a 1992 document, *An Open and Structured Dialogue between the Commission and Special Interest Groups*, the European Commission began to explore its relationship with interest groups, both non-profit and profit-making organizations. The document followed on from the Galle Report which had raised concerns that the democratic process was being hijacked by the garish behaviour of some lobbyists within the EU institutions (McLaughlin and Greenwood, 1995). The Galle Report called for better regulation of interest representation in order to prevent abuses, greater transparency and improved access for non-profit groups to the EU policymaking process. This report, as well as the policy document by the Commission that followed, were written at the same time as the negotiations for the Treaty of the European Union (Maastricht Treaty) were taking place in 1991–2. An underlining goal of the Treaty of EU was to develop a more open community that would benefit from a more informed public debate, and this document reflects the thought processes that tried to operationalize this aim.

The purpose of the 1992 communication from the Commission was therefore to spark a long-term discussion on the role of civil society actors in the workings of the EU, soliciting input from academics and professionals familiar with these issues. It recognized the value of special interest groups as a 'channel to provide specific technical expertise' (European Commission, 1992, p. 1). Describing the dialogue with these groups as 'valuable', the communication set out to further formalize the relationship and in so doing make the engagement process more transparent. Increased transparency in EU operations, the document argued, would ensure a more informed public debate on its activities. It recalls the Maastricht Treaty that had been recently signed, and which states that 'transparency of the decision-making process strengthens the democratic nature of the institutions and the public's confidence in the administration' (European Commission, 1992, p. 2). Even at this early stage the value of civil society engagement is articulated in terms of contributions made to policy effectiveness and democratization.

The second document titled *Communication from the Commission on Promoting the Role of Voluntary Organizations and Foundations in Europe*, published in 1997, develops the argumentation further and pursues the idea of civil dialogue as a means to achieve greater social solidarity and citizenship (European Commission, 1997; Finke, 2007; Smismans, 2003). This communication is similar to the one discussed before, in that its publication coincided with the ratification of the Treaty of Amsterdam in 1997, which set out the principles of liberal democracy that the EU would adhere to: respect for human rights and fundamental freedoms, rule of law and liberty (Greenwood, 2007). The document therefore offers a strong indication of how this broad debate on democratic principles was to be interpreted as far as policy towards civil society was concerned.

Here civil society is for the first time considered separately from profit-making organizations that have a similar relationship with EU institutions. The document also recognizes the role of civil society in creating jobs, demonstrating active citizenship and exercising democracy. These actions make a contribution to European integration; as the communication argues:

> For many people, membership of, or volunteering for, voluntary organizations and foundations, provides a vital means through which they can express their sense of citizenship, and demonstrate an active concern for their fellows and for society at large [...] foster a sense of solidarity and of citizenship, and provide the essential underpinnings of our democracy [...] providing

citizens with the means with which they may critically examine government actions or proposals.

European Commission (1997, pp. 4–7)

The document suggests that there are linkages between certain civil societal activities and the development of social solidarity, citizenship and democracy. By providing adequate means for civil society to participate in governmental decision-making processes, it is possible to foster such behaviour, the document contends, and in so doing enhance the democratic character of European society. The democratic value of civil society is therefore linked to certain behaviour by civil society. In these policy documents, the idea of civil society becomes subsumed under a category of particular activities and outcomes. The activities related to consultation are linked with certain outcomes such as a better sense of solidarity, increased participation in democratic processes and improved policy effectiveness. Citizen participation in shaping government policy is seen as a way of expressing a democratic voice. The motivations to pursue a greater relationship with civil society are based on improved policy efficacy and enhanced democratic processes. In 1998, the EU began to prepare for the eventual enlargement into Eastern European countries by gradually opening the accession negotiations with the ten new member states that would join in May 2004. As the following two documents point out, the impending enlargement generates an additional focus for EU's civil society policy. The first document, from the year 2000, illustrates a new, more carefully thought-out list of activities for cooperating with NGOs, which reflect the newfound challenges of enlargement and integration. The second document, a white paper from 2001, demonstrates how the development of civil society is deemed an integral part of the accession process for the Eastern European candidate countries.

A methodical and detailed consideration of the EU–civil society relationship appeared in the year 2000 in the form of a Commission discussion paper, *The Commission and Non-Governmental Organizations: Building a Stronger Partnership* (European Commission, 2000). The document recognizes the ever-increasing number of NGOs operating within and outside of Europe and acknowledges the need to develop a more structured framework for managing the relationships between NGOs and EU institutions. It offers a five-point rationale for cooperating with NGOs, which includes 'fostering participatory democracy', 'contributing to policymaking' and 'contributing to European integration' (European Commission, 2000, pp. 3–4). Although much of the document is dedicated to technical, managerial and budgetary details of how EU grants to NGOs should operate, one section titled 'Dialogue and Consultation' discusses how the broader strategy that the Commission envisions will be taken forward:

> Dialogue and consultation between NGOs and the Commission have to be seen in the framework of the democratic decision-making process of the European institutions [...] dialogue between the European Commission and NGOs is an important complement to the institutional process of policy-shaping.
>
> European Commission (2000, p. 7)

These comments reiterate the policy logic outlined earlier, and demonstrate how the backbone of the EU logic to civil society engagement began to crystallize. It is based on policy effectiveness and democracy-enhancing characteristics of NGOs. Greenwood describes these two sides of the policy coin as input and output legitimacy (2007; cf. Scharpf, 1999). Input legitimacy draws on the genuine preferences of citizens, while output legitimacy is based on results and policy outcomes. The central point is that part of the rationale for the EU's engagement with civil society views NGOs as a useful vehicle in generating input and output legitimacy. NGOs are thus a useful instrument that will help with broader dilemmas of governance that the EU faces.

The 2001 *White Paper on European Governance* is regarded as a milestone in the development of the EU's relationship with civil society (Finke, 2007; Greenwood, 2007). This document is concerned with the lack of public confidence in the European institutions – such as the EU parliament, the EU commission and Council of Ministers – because they are complex and poorly understood. To tackle this concern, the paper posits the idea of 'good governance' consisting of openness, participation, accountability, effectiveness and coherence (European Commission, 2001). By opening up the policymaking process, the document argues, European institutions can regain the confidence of the public. Civil society plays a central role in this:

> Civil society plays an important role in giving voice to the concerns of citizens and delivering services that meet people's

needs [...] The organizations which make up civil society mobilise people and support, for instance, those suffering from exclusion or discrimination. The Union has encouraged the development of civil society in the applicant countries, as part of their preparation for membership.

European Commission (2001)

The document presents two reasons to engage with civil society actors. First, civil society makes a real contribution to the delivery of social services. This is seen to be a good thing and one that should be supported. Second, they can amplify the democratic noise at the EU level, by mobilizing citizens, and by giving a voice to people who would otherwise be unable to make their opinions heard. By listening to civil society, it may be possible to alleviate some of the concerns people have about a democratic deficit at the level of EU governance. Hence more civil society means both better services and better democracy. The document reflects a genuine interest in the potential contribution civil society can make to improved governance. Bottom-up involvement and consulting civil society were also the two areas that drew most positive interests from the public, according to a follow-up report commissioned on European governance (European Commission, 2003a, p. 8). The previous quotation is also interesting for the reference it makes to EU candidate countries. There is an effortless shift from the internal EU context to issues that exist outside of these borders. In other words, there is an expectation that civil society in a candidate country operates – or ought to operate – in a similar fashion to how it does within the EU. This prescribes a particular type as the correct form of civil society, and this is what should be aspired to in applicant countries. It paves the way for Europeanization processes to unfold in ways congruent with this view of what civil society means.

Policy characteristics

Moving on now from looking at reasons for civil society engagement to investigating how it is engaged, at the EU level, the motivation for involving CSOs originates largely from a desire to improve its own decision-making and policymaking capacities. The policy measures circulate around two keywords: consultation and dialogue. The benefits of increased consultation are argued in terms of the improvements this would bring to policy design and in terms of the enhanced efficiencies that would result from this. Dialogue, on the other hand, is perceived primarily to facilitate a two-way dissemination of information. Through this dialogue information travels both downstream, through CSOs to European citizens, as well as upstream, ensuring that grass-roots experiences are taken into account. It reflects concern for both input and output legitimacy.

These roles resonate with the concept of third sector. As discussed elsewhere, third sector thinking combines the best of two worlds – the efficiency of the private sector and the accountability of government. Bringing CSOs into the mix offers a more diverse set of service providers as well as new points of view at the policy table. The language of consultation expects CSOs to meet on a level playing field with either national or European-level actors and to have the capacity to communicate their ideas effectively at this level. It is only a large professional organization that is able to undertake such a role. In addition, the language of dialogue suggests a close bond, even like-mindedness, between those that are working together. The notion of dialogue assumes that the parties in dialogue are not in total disagreement, as it is the resolution of differences that is the expected end result of a dialogue. All in all, the policy characteristics offer opportunities to a narrow field of actors who are already operating near the firmament of civil society.

EU civil society policy in the Mediterranean context

In the last two decades the Mediterranean region has become an increasingly important partner in the EU's external policy (Crawford, 1998). In 1997, the Treaty of Amsterdam was ratified, making democracy and human rights a central objective of EU external policy and contributing to this shift in the direction of funding (Brandtner and Rosas, 1998). This is also the context in which EU policy has employed the idea of civil society in external context. The current section will address this question from the point of view of a wider EU policy towards civil society in the Mediterranean region. In the years preceding Turkey's accession negotiations, EU civil society development projects in Turkey were operated from within the MEDA programme,[2] which was designed to help the Mediterranean non-member countries to reform their economic and social structures.

Democratic reform is at the heart of EU's more recent policy towards the Mediterranean region,[3] although the suitability of this approach has come under question. In a recent assessment, for example, Roderick Pace has argued that there are benefits to reforms that set up free market economies as they create irresistible pressures to establish democratic political institutions. However, most countries in the region accept the reforms advocating economic liberalism, but resist democratic reforms. This resistance is a pragmatic response by a political elite clinging to power, not evidence of a fundamental clash between different cultural principles (Islamic) and liberal democracy. Pace does not suggest, therefore, that EU policy is doomed to fail regardless of the form its policies take, but rather that in its current form the policy misunderstands the regional context by assuming a causal relationship between liberal economic policies and democratization.

Nor has EU policy been particularly consistent. In comparing the application of the democracy rhetoric between EU efforts to promote civil society in Africa and the Middle East, Gordon Crawford has noted significant differences in its application. The EU has been much more forgiving with Middle Eastern countries' resistance to democratic reform. This, he argues, has to do with the instrumental (as opposed to normative) approach to democracy that is pursued by EU policy. Political stability is regarded as more important than full-fledged democratization (Crawford, 2007, p. 183). The pragmatic aim of EU policy is, he argues, to create a slimmer bureaucracy, leaving the authoritarian political elite in its place. Others, however, argue that it is necessary to move beyond considerations of how external actors can influence democratization processes, and to focus on the possible contributions of domestic actors (Pace, Seeberg and Cavatorta, 2009). Capturing the debates about EU policy and the particular visions of democracy embedded within it are important, but are only able to offer a limited explanation of how these policies are captured and implemented by local actors. The relationships are not unidirectional and the EU is not necessarily the dominant partner (Pace, Seeberg and Cavatorta, 2009, pp. 7–8).

The Barcelona Process

EU policy towards the Mediterranean region has become crystallized in the Euro-Mediterranean Partnership, commonly known as the Barcelona Process. Established in the slipstream of the Barcelona Declaration in 1995, the Barcelona Process has focused on improving relations with the non-EU member states of the Mediterranean (European Commission, 2008). The documents detailing this process state the key goals to be 'the creation of an area of peace and stability based on fundamental principles, including respect for human rights and democracy' (European Commission, 2008, p. 2). The same document comments further that to 'promote principles such as modernization, participation, equality, human rights, democracy and good governance and the ability to act freely within civil society' are a fundamental part of this goal (European Commission, 2007a, p. 58).

More recent policy developments have pushed the democracy and human rights aspect of this partnership even further, at the same time making civil society more central to the process. In 2003 the European Commission issued a Communication titled *Reinvigorating EU Actions on Human Rights and Democratization with Mediterranean Partners – Strategic Guidelines* (European Commission, 2003b). As the title suggests, the document identifies a need to find ways to breathe new life into EU's democracy-building efforts in the region. It calls for democratization and human rights promotion to be prioritized within EU external policy and for a proactive approach to be adopted (European Commission, 2003b). Furthermore, according to the document, democracy and human rights should constitute the core objectives of EU's external policy – after all, these are the same principles upon which the EU itself has been founded. These examples strongly suggest that experiences of democracy from within the EU are heavily informing the expectations of how its external policy of democracy promotion should shape out. The role of civil society is largely at the centre of these external expectations as NGOs are asked to take a greater role in the implementation and monitoring of EU human rights and democratization policies in the region. The value of NGOs is understood to be in their 'effectiveness in identifying problems and lobbying for improvements' (European Commission, 2003b, p. 13). The problems in the Mediterranean region are particularly acute for NGOs that practice advocacy or work in the field of human rights as they 'face legal and administrative constraints, are frequently marginalised and sometimes repressed' (European Commission, 2003b, p. 4).

The Barcelona Process has initiated a range of programmes that aim directly towards civil societal development, each of which funds several projects.[4] 'TRESMED – Civil Society Dialogue' is one telling programme. It aims to provide a framework for dialogue in an effort to support civil society, good governance and democratization. In particular the project aims to strengthen the consultative role of civil society, encouraging participation in political decision-making processes (European Commission, 2007a, p. 72). The programme activities consist of NGO training, study visits, seminars and networking. By giving social and economic actors a voice, the objective of the programme is to support civil society, good governance and democratization.

In the context of the Barcelona Process, EU policy has embraced civil society by pursuing improved standards of human rights and democracy, and by engaging civil society actors in a dialogue. CSOs are valued for their work in lobbying governments for improvements as well as for implementing and monitoring democratization and human rights policies. The language explaining the policy shift describes it as a way to better align EU external policy with EU's internal values of democracy and human rights. It is not surprising to see that civil society is expected to contribute to democratization, improve standards of human rights and increase social dialogue as per the internal experience within the EU. The democratic value of civil society arises from its role in policy consultation with governments, and the projects in the Mediterranean region aspire to this also.

Thus, across the two contexts there is considerable overlap between the underlying premises as to what civil society is expected to do. On the one hand greater civil society involvement can improve the efficacy of other EU policies in the region. On the other hand, civil society can promote democracy by channelling the concerns of citizens to the higher echelons. It seems, therefore, that the EU is on a mission to export a particular style of civil society activism that has more resonance with the European vision of civil society as third sector, and where CSOs play the dual role of providing services and deepening democratic practices. But who are the civil society actors with sufficient capacity to perform these roles in a developing country context?

EU civil society policy in the Turkish context

This section looks more closely at the justifications given for EU involvement in civil society activity in Turkey. In October 2004, the European Commission published a document which contained the broad framework for Turkey's accession process. The document titled *Recommendation of the European Commission on Turkey's Progress towards Accession* highlights two policy streams where civil society is given a prominent role. First, civil society has an important role in reinforcing and supporting the political reform process that is taking place in Turkey, alluding to initiatives that aim to strengthen democracy in Turkey by funding NGOs. The second one is a package of initiatives delivered in support of a process titled Civil Society Dialogue, referring to a need to strengthen the dialogue between Turkey and the EU on a number of issues, including the differences of cultures, religion, issues relating to migration, concerns on minority rights and terrorism. The document goes as far as stating that 'civil society should play the most important role in this dialogue' (European Commission, 2004a, p. 8).

As before, there are many similarities between the policy language found in documents concerning EU's internal policy towards civil society and those that describe the support for Turkish civil society. It should be noted that this is not wholly unexpected, given that the policy aims are closely related to the broader aim of Turkey's eventual EU accession. Nevertheless, the question of how realistic it is to expect Turkish civil society actors to behave in a way that supports these aims remains legitimate.

Policy stream 1: Democracy

> To join the EU, a new Member State must [achieve] stability of institutions guaranteeing democracy, the rule of law, human rights and respect for and protection of minorities.
>
> European Union (2009)

The democratic guidelines included in the accession criteria are possibly the most important (and certainly the most prominent) theme for reform that the Turkish government faces with regard to Turkey's EU membership. The centrality of democratic development to the EU accession process is laid out by the first of three pillars that together make up the Copenhagen Criteria that have formed the conditions of entry for all candidate countries since 1999. This pillar outlines stable democratic institutions, rule of law, human rights and protection of minorities as prerequisites for accession. The second pillar expects Turkey to develop and maintain a functioning market economy with the capacity to cope with market forces within the EU. The third pillar requires Turkey to comply with the Community *acquis* (the total body of EU law). Within this three-pronged approach, the role of civil society in the accession process is largely framed around the first pillar, around the issues of democracy and human rights. A look at the rationales that accompany EU projects shows how they are often justified on the basis of their contribution to democratization. Three such project rationales will be analysed with the intention of explicating what the EU visualizes the contribution of civil society to be, demonstrating that the EU regards Turkish civil society as a fundamental constituent of Turkey's democratic development.

The first example is from a project on 'Improving Co-operation between the NGOs and the Public Sector and Strengthening the NGOs Democratic Participation Level'. The dual objective set out by the project title fits neatly within the process of aligning Turkey's domestic institutional framework with those of the EU. In order to achieve these aims, the project aims to create and implement an 'action plan on the public sector – civil society cooperation'. The emphasis will be on achieving cooperation through a structured dialogue between NGOs and the public sector, as an improved relationship between the two is seen as a required outcome of the pre-accession phase (European Commission, 2003c, pp. 1–2). Indeed, the project objectives are consciously and consistently aligned with the aims of the accession process:

> A well-developed and functioning civil society is an essential element of a democratic system and efficient NGOs have a key role to play in expressing the demands of citizens by encouraging their active participation as well as raising their awareness. Furthermore, many elements of the *acquis communautaire* are based on the existence of operational NGOs operating within the related policy area.
>
> European Commission (2003c, p. 2)

The two reasons that are given for why this project is necessary can be summarized as 'it is good for democracy' and 'it is required by the accession process'. Structured dialogue between NGOs and the public sector is desirable because it increases the democratic participation levels of NGOs and because this dialogue improves ties between civil society and public sector. Elements of the EU law (*acquis*) anticipate the existence of NGOs that act in a certain way, and contribute to the policy process in a certain way. If Turkey is to successfully comply with the accession criteria, it needs to have NGOs fulfilling these roles. The project documentation in fact admits that certain types of NGO relationships and activities are encouraged because this is the way in which things are done within in the EU.

The second example is a project titled 'Strengthening Freedom of Association for Further Development of Civil Society'. The overall objective is stated as 'enhanced participatory democracy through strengthened NGOs'. This is to be achieved by increasing NGO capacity for 'networking, voluntary work, national and international dialogue in Turkey' (European Commission, 2004a, p. 1). The justification for the project is based on the requirements of the first pillar of the Copenhagen Criteria. The activities perceived by the project are broken down into three components. The first component includes capacity-building for NGOs through comprehensive training in organizational management. The second component comprises raising awareness of civil society among NGOs, media, public authorities and general public by establishing a communication centre and by promoting the NGO sector through seminars, conferences and publications. The third component offers micro-grants to NGOs in order to facilitate dialogue and communication with their counterparts in the EU (European Commission, 2004a, p. 5).

The third sample project is called 'Strengthening Civil Society in the Pre-accession Process' and aims to 'contribute to the consolidation and broadening of political reforms and EU alignment efforts through strengthening the civil society in Turkey in the pre-accession process' (European Commission, 2005). The first component of the project offers grants to various rights-based pursuits in the areas of women's rights, disability rights, consumer rights, child rights and environmental activism. The second component provides funds to activities that consolidate human rights and democracy, combat violence against women or contribute to the engagement of the Turkish public in the accession process (European Commission, 2005). In each of these areas the document goes on to provide further justification for civil society funding by outlining the current weaknesses in civil society activity in each area, and expressing a desire to develop this further. This is desirable because it helps to consolidate the ongoing reforms and the currently underdeveloped role of civil society in each of the aforementioned areas. Through these developments Turkey will move a step closer to EU membership, the document suggests (European Commission, 2005, p. 28).

During the years leading up to the start of the accession process (2004), efforts at democratization were at the heart of EU civil society-building efforts in Turkey. Project funding supporting rights-based initiatives, encouraging networking between NGOs by way of strengthening their common voice, and improving relations between NGOs and the public sector were some of the areas where democratization was being pursued by the aforementioned projects. From 2004 onwards, the attention of civil society policy has gradually moved in another direction.

Policy stream 2: Dialogue

> [A]ny future enlargement of the EU needs to be supported by a strong, deep and sustained dialogue [...] this would help to bridge the information gap, achieve better mutual knowledge and bring citizens and different cultures, political and economic systems closer together, thus ensuring a stronger awareness of the opportunities as well as challenges of future accessions [...] *civil society should play the most important role in this dialogue.*
>
> European Union (2005, p. 2)

The next phase of the EU–civil society relationship – the idea of civil society dialogue – was first proposed in October 2004 by the European Commission and endorsed by the European Council in December 2004 (European Commission, 2004b). Incidentally, parallel to this, on 17 December 2004 the European Union agreed to initiate the accession negotiations with Turkey. Then in June 2005 – four months before the first six chapters of the *acquis* were opened for negotiations in October – a communication titled *Civil Society Dialogue between the EU and Candidate Countries* was published by the European Commission that spells out the nature of the policy shift this innovation brings along with it. In the context of the accession process the dialogue stream has gradually taken over from the democratization stream as the central theme of civil society funding (although, as will be shown, the two remain interlinked). The document claims to draw on the lessons learnt from previous rounds of enlargement and, it seems highly probable, was written with Turkey's accession negotiations specifically in mind.[5]

The emergence of civil society dialogue represents an important policy shift that further centralizes the role of civil society in the accession process. For example, the communication earmarks as much as 8–10 per cent of Turkey's total annual financial assistance to civil society-related activities (European Union, 2005, p. 14). Drawing on the rational choice framework, a new kind of rational calculus entered the EU–Turkey relationship with the advent of the membership negotiations. Funding for civil society shifted away from addressing Turkey's democratic and political shortcomings directly and focused primarily on facilitating the accession process. The aim of this dialogue is to make sure that both Turkish and EU citizens are sufficiently informed about the other prior to accession. The more efforts there are at exchanging ideas across the EU–Turkey borders, the more ideological cleavages can be bridged and differences of opinion ironed out. NGOs are seen as key agents within this process of dialogue, asked to facilitate the accession process by way of establishing a channel of communication between the two sides in the negotiations. The document goes on to outline further aims as well. This dialogue, by way of increasing the participation of civil society in political, cultural and economic development, is also seen to develop 'a lively and vibrant civil society in candidate countries, which is a key to the consolidation of human rights and democracy' (European Union, 2005, p. 4). This new policy therefore is also seen to continue the democratizing efforts by the EU.

The most extensive and comprehensive commitment to increased civil society dialogue has come in the form of a broad, new grant programme. 'Promotion of the Civil Society Dialogue between Turkey and the European Union' ran from 2006 to December 2009 and committed to awarding grants amounting to €19.3 million in total. The grants were divided across four separate schemes: Towns and Municipalities (€5 million), Professional Organizations (€3 million), Universities (€9.3 million) and Youth Initiatives for

Dialogue (€2 million). In total, 119 projects have been awarded grants, and in each case a Turkish organization has partnered with an organization from an EU member state or another candidate country (Civil Society Dialogue Project, 2009).

The programme aims to strengthen contacts and the exchange of experiences between civil society in the EU and Turkey, and to ensure better understanding on both sides of the history, culture and values of the other (European Commission, 2006b, p. 1). The development of civil society dialogue with Turkey is underlined by an expectation that this will contribute to a better-informed public opinion, encourage discussion on culture and values, and facilitate the sharing of experiences across the EU–Turkey border. These outcomes are expected to increase civil society participation in the political, cultural and economic development of Turkey, and to aid in the 'development of a lively and vibrant civil society, which is key to the consolidation of democracy' (European Commission, 2006b, pp. 4–5). There is a distinct instrumental undertone to these projects that sees NGOs as vehicles that aim to deliver rather specific outcomes.

The following section considers one of these four grant schemes in closer detail, namely the Youth Initiatives for Dialogue scheme. The objectives for this scheme follow the broader programme aims outlined previously. The two central aims of the grant are the following:

(1) To promote mutually beneficial and sustainable relationships between youth initiatives in Turkey and in EU member states and candidate countries and promote dialogue between the Turkish and EU counterparts by addressing the opportunities and challenges of enlargement.
(2) To encourage exchange of knowledge and best practices on planning and implementation of EU policies (EUSG, 2009).

These objectives utilize civil society as an instrument in the accession process. The participating youth groups are expected, through their involvement in the project, to address issues concerning EU enlargement. There is an expectation that the funding will facilitate a learning process that directly helps the accession process. This, when compared with the earlier funding framework that concentrated on democratization, represents a clear shift in EU civil society policy.

The funding is granted for projects that are between €30,000 and €100,000 in value, and this leads to further consequences for participating NGOs. At most, 90 per cent of the total costs of the project are covered by the grant. In other words, in order to qualify for a grant the recipient must have at least €3000 in cash or have secured funding from another non-EU source (EUSG, 2009). Together, these requirements limit potential applicants because, given the relatively high value of the grants, it is likely that any successful applicant will have had previous experience of managing a funded project. The requirement for alternate sources of funding acts as a similar limitation; a successful candidate is required to have sufficient capacity to look for two sources of funding at the same time. Consequently the funding is channelled towards the large, established organizations that are able to manage the process successfully.

Finally, all projects are required to incorporate two kinds of compulsory activities. First, to organize information campaigns and events, such as seminars and conferences, and to engage wider community groups with these activities. Second, projects are required to include actions and events that promote the project and ensure the visibility of EU support and the concept of civil society dialogue (EUSG, 2009). In effect, the participating NGOs are treated as an extension of a marketing campaign for EU enlargement. Civil society is here seen as a partner that has been asked to deliver specific outcomes that suit EU needs in terms of Turkey's broader accession process.

Although one could argue that the requirements EU projects make are in fact reasonable, given that the funding comes from taxpayers who expect the money to be spent effectively, it is also important to consider the extent to which this style of funding complements the end goals of the funding, such as democratization and dialogue between NGOs. As Chapter 6 illustrates, this type of funding contributes to the development of a two-tier civil society between those that are able to gain access to funding and those that are not. Moreover, Chapter 7 highlights the issue of NGOs gaining access to EU funding with the help of consultancy firms that write the applications, while the NGOs itself lacks the capacity to deliver the projects competently.

Conclusion

In exploring the evolution of EU policies towards civil society in the second section, 'EU policy towards civil society, 1992–2003', two broad conclusions were made. First, working with CSOs was justified because they were able to deliver important services to society and thus support governments in serving their citizens. Second, CSOs were deemed valuable because they were able to enhance the democratic qualities of a society by providing an avenue through which citizens could make their voices heard. Moreover, the very act of delivering services through CSOs was seen as democracy-enhancing. This thinking crystallized around two policy objectives. The first objective was to consult CSOs during the policymaking process in order to improve the effectiveness and efficiency of policies. The second objective aimed to start a dialogue that leads to a two-way dissemination of information.

These policy aspirations have much in common with the theoretical premise introduced by Ferguson, Hegel and de Tocqueville in the previous chapter. Civil society is seen as a useful facilitator between the market economy and the state, while at the same time retaining independence from the two. Shadowing de Tocqueville's argument about the democratic value of civil society, the independence also makes civil society a useful ally in democratization efforts, as it enables civil society actors to question the state and ensure it remains accountable to its citizens. Such qualities make civil society a key component of a successful modern system of governance.

The EU-led civil society initiatives inside and outside its borders are strikingly similar to each other. Although EU democracy promotion policies in the Mediterranean and Turkey have focused less on engaging CSOs in consultations on government decision-making by supporting groups (such as rights-based NGOs) who make their critique of government policy heard through more informal means, the EU clearly has a very similar end goal in mind. The similarities in the policies, and in the language supporting these policies, indicate that the EU regards the application of the concept in universal fashion across different contexts as unproblematic. It is a neutral, technical policy exercise in how to engage civil society in a constructive manner. For the EU, civil society is an instrument that can aid in realizing their policy goals as well as a structure that is believed to function in a sufficiently similar manner across various cultural contexts.

How useful is it to have this kind of uniformity in policymaking? Some would advocate that we should continue to see policy as a rational and technical process, and formulate policy goals on the basis that it satisfies certain minimum requirements. Others argue that we ought to pursue a more individualistic understanding of the consequence of policy, and consider more carefully the politics of the policy process. In the case of the EU and Turkey, these policies can be conceived of as aiming for Europeanization, that is, processes broadly defined as political, policy, societal or discursive change towards the European mainstream.

The lens of historical institutionalism offers one way of explaining the uniformity in policy. Since the early 1990s, the EU has incrementally set out a strategy for engaging with civil society where each policy document built on the logic of the one preceding it. With each policy document, the selected policy approach gathers greater mass and reduces the space for alternative approaches to develop. In a sense, what the chronology of policy documents in this chapter charts is the gradual increase in institutional inertia, making alternative approaches less likely. This policy trajectory then forms the framework within which processes of policy Europeanization take place during Turkey's accession negotiations also.

Additionally, the lens of rational choice institutionalism can help to explain the emergence of civil society dialogue as the new funding strategy, replacing the earlier policy of supporting rights-based NGOs directly. Although the stated aims of civil society dialogue – democratization and building of vibrant civil society – have not completely changed from what they were previously, the manner in which this is to be achieved has. The assumption that actors' behaviour is governed by a 'strategic calculus' (Hall and Taylor, 1996) would suggest that the policy shift towards civil society dialogue would incur lower political costs for incumbent governments and would therefore achieve improved compliance from governments. The policy on civil society dialogue has been framed differently from previous frameworks, in that it is less confrontational. NGO actions, as far as the project domain is concerned, have been tamed by projects that fund the less confrontational activities.

However, the subsequent chapters question the extent to which the aforesaid understanding of how Europeanization processes unfold is in fact supported by evidence. NGO funding has been increasingly engulfed by Europeanization, and what follows investigates how NGO actors have experienced the effect of these processes and how they have reacted in response. The issues covered range from the nature of short-term project funding and complexity of accounting procedures to the introduction of domestic governmental actors as the new gatekeepers of EU civil society funds. The discrepancies between the content and implementation of EU civil society policy and the everyday experiences and practices of NGOs generate tension and dissatisfaction among the NGO community. As Chapter 7 demonstrates, these discrepancies also generate space for NGOs to develop coping strategies and opportunities for 'benign manipulation' of project funding, leading to different policy outcomes from what was intended.

4
Civil Society in Turkey

This chapter provides a contextual background on the development of civil society in Turkey, and in so doing acts as a hinge between the theoretical and policy debates of the previous chapters and the empirical discussion of the subsequent chapters. It endeavours to highlight the relevance of historical context in explaining how certain idiosyncrasies regarding the development of civil society have arisen in Turkey. In particular, the chapter explores the historical bifurcation of civil society into 'official' (secular, nationalist voices) and 'informal' (non-secular, minority voices) sectors, and its consequences on the development of civil society in Turkey. Although somewhat crude as a distinction, this division remains a useful heuristic device to describe the outcomes of the radical modernization and Westernization processes instigated in the early years of the Turkish republic. The last three decades have seen tremendous growth in the size and role of civil society in Turkey, as well as in the variety of organizational forms. Yet the attitudes underlying the earlier bifurcation still resonate in present-day relationships within civil society, particularly within the critical debates on issues such as the role of religion in Turkish politics and society.

Civil society in Turkey today is both heterogeneous and fragmented. These mixed dynamics, between the old black-and-white divisions and the new, increasingly multifarious character of civil society place Turkey into an unknown territory, where the opportunities offered by democratization and EU accession mix with the shortcomings that arise from the social divisions that still continue to exist in Turkish civil society. These political dynamics contribute to the unpredictable and uncertain nature of Europeanization and civil society development in Turkey. I argue that these developments have had, broadly speaking, an enabling effect on civil society. The EU has provided an external anchor for the claims NGOs have made, and by taking NGO activity seriously, the EU has legitimized their actions in the eyes of the public. However, at the same time we need to understand the limitations.

The chapter consists of four sections. The first part turns the clock back to a time when the ideas of the modern Turkish nation were first being formulated. The principles behind the modern republic and Turkish nation state-building created certain challenges in the way of civil societal development. The situation, however, has undergone some far-reaching changes since the 1980s, and the impact of this transposition is the focus of the second section. In this period new, autonomous civil societal voices of all colours began to emerge, representing a break with the bifurcated divisions of the past. Section three considers the impact of the EU accession process on the development of civil society. Efforts at Europeanization of Turkey and Turkish civil society underpin this section, as it looks at how domestic politics have responded to the opportunities and challenges delivered by the Europeanizing forces that have been in play since the late 1980s. The final section explores the actors and recent events in Turkish civil society in more detail, beginning with an outline of how secular and Islamic camps have elected to position themselves in the currents of Europeanization.

The Turkish paradox

The Turkish Republic that emerged in the 1920s continued the gargantuan task of turning the remnants of the Ottoman Empire into a modern, Westernized nation state. The emergent republic searched for a compromise between the Ottoman traditions that drew on Islamic history and culture and the far-reaching secular reforms that drastically broke away from this. The solution was to pursue the modernization agenda in areas such as politics, law and governance, while in the spiritual, cultural and ethical domains Islamic traditions continued to flourish (as long as this did not interfere with the processes of modernization). What emerged, then, was a public–private divide where politics, law and governance were within the public realm and religion was pushed out of the public and into the private realm. Many observers refer to this compromise as an apparent 'paradox' in the development logic of the Turkish republic because the aim of significantly limiting religion as a public, political force remained alien to large swathes of the population (Kadioğlu, 1996; Keyman, 1995; Kubicek, 1999; Parla, 1985; Yavuz, 2003; Yilmaz, 2007). From this paradox emerge the later political tensions that continue to shape Turkish politics even today. Civil society was employed in managing this paradox, leading to a bifurcated, two-tier civil society where a relatively narrow band of organizations that were secular-minded or nationalist in their outlook was given scope to grow. This left other civil society actors to fend for themselves without state support (and often facing active state interference).

'Turkish-Islamist-Westernist Modernism' as a formula for reform

The ideas of Ziya Gökalp mark a starting point for an outline of the journey that Turkish civil society has taken since the formation of the Turkish Republic. Gökalp (1876–1924) was a political philosopher from the Ottoman era who was among the early advocates of Turkish nationalism. In the post-Ottoman era his ideas became influential among the new elite, as it was reconceptualizing the path a modern Turkish Republic ought to take and his unique contribution was a synthesis of a number of theoretical strands that together possessed a powerful resonance with the future direction of Turkey. His theory titled 'Turkist-Islamist-Westernist Modernism' gave each of these notions a role in society: 'We are of the Turkish nation (*millet*), of the Islamic religious community (*ümmet*), of Western civilization (*medeniyet*)' (Parla, 1985).

It seemed highly paradoxical to attempt to synthesize the Western and Islamic traditions in this way. The scientific and technological innovation of the West was somehow to be balanced with the spirituality of the East (Kadioğlu, 1996, p. 719; Parla, 1985). To reconcile the irreconcilable, and to resolve the paradox, he went on to make a distinction between culture and civilization. Culture, Gökalp argued, should remain intrinsic to Turkey and retain a domestic origin, while the ingredients for civilization could be borrowed from outside. In so doing it would be possible to adopt Western institutions, values and norms so far as they were necessary for acquiring a modern, civilized society, while concurrently protecting traditional, national values from an outside influence (Kubicek, 1999; Parla, 1985). In practice, however, the synthesis has led to an unstable compromise where tensions periodically mount between the modernizing reformists (secular) and traditionalists who resist change (Islamist).

Gökalp's ideas were a significant source of inspiration for the founder of the modern Turkish Republic and its first president, Mustafa Kemal Atatürk. Atatürk pursued an energetic reform agenda that adopted many of the Western values and norms on the one hand, while establishing the groundwork for a homogeneous, Turkish national identity on the other. In pursuit of civilizational reforms, the Turkish Republic adopted the Latin script; the fez was banned in favour of a European-style headgear; the *Sharia* law was replaced by a legal code modelled on European examples; and as early as 1930 women were given the right to vote in municipal elections, a right that was extended to national elections in 1934 (Poulton, 1997).[1] The mould used to establish a modern Turkish civilization was distinctly European. Above all, the process of secularization was what defined the paradigm shift that was taking place. The highest political authority in Sunni Islam that functioned as a united voice for the Muslim Ummah, the Caliphate, was abolished. These powers were transferred to the newly established parliament, the Grand National Assembly of Turkey (Dodd, 1992). Not only were relations between religion and state severed, but Islam was nationalized by way of establishing the Directorate of Religious Affairs (*Diyanet İşleri Başkanlığı*), a state institution which to this day retains a regulatory oversight over all Muslim religious activities in Turkey (Yilmaz, 2007). These reforms imported secular measures that seemed to bode well for the further development of civil society. It would be less likely that public issues, such as women's rights, would be curtailed on the grounds that they belonged to the domain of religion and were therefore not open to public debate.

However, the extent to which the social fabric of Turkey was being ripped apart by the reforms meant the politicians and policymakers behind the programme had to be in total control in order to ensure the reforms were carried out. This in turn limited the possibilities for certain parts of civil society to grow. Thus the question asked was not 'who are the Turks' but rather 'who are the Turks going to be'

(Kadioğlu, 1996, p. 179). The reforms were not an expression of an existing national consciousness, but rather an abstract construction that broke away from religiously or ethnically constructed models. The ideas of a Turkish nation and a republican state became virtually synonymous, where social forces that deviated from the republican norms (but were otherwise legitimate) were squeezed out from public discussion (Seufert, 2000). The reform process interpreted the general will in a very particular way.

Another element of the paradox arises from Turkey's ambivalent attitudes towards Westernization. The desire to build a modern Turkish state in the image of Western civilizations has been counterpoised by a deep-seated suspicion of the West. This ambivalent attitude has become coined as the 'Sèvres Syndrome'. Although the Treaty of Sèvres, drawn up by the Allied powers in 1920 following the end of the First World War, was later nullified, it remains as a reminder in the Turkish social consciousness of the potential untrustworthiness of the West. In addition to the secession of Ottoman territories in the Middle East, the treaty divided most of present-day Turkey into zones of influence between the Allied forces, Greece and Armenia, leaving central Anatolia and the Black Sea region in the north as independent. These terms were deemed wholly unacceptable and formed one key determinant mobilizing a series of guerrilla wars against the occupying forces, which culminated in the national resistance led by Mustafa Kemal and the War of Independence (1919–23). The end result was the Treaty of Lausanne, which annulled the earlier Treaty of Sèvres and recognized the present-day borders of Turkey. The lesson learnt from this experience, argues Hakan Yilmaz, was that the Europeans saw Turks as illegitimate occupiers of lands that rightfully belonged to European-Christian people (Yilmaz, 2006). Since then, the Sèvres Syndrome has crystallized into two policy imperatives: isolationism (never trust Western states or enter into economic, political or cultural pacts) and Westernization without the West (modernize the state, military, economy and the society but never lose sight of the importance of isolationism) (Yilmaz, 2006, p. 36). The nationalist and anti-Western attitudes, therefore, sat uneasily with the cosmopolitan civilizational agenda that looked to the West for inspiration. These mixed attitudes continue to inform the political debate around the processes of Europeanization and how the accession negotiations in general are interpreted.

Modernization and a two-tier civil society

The resultant national identity was premised on secular Turkishness, forming a rather narrow overlap with other existing identities. Society was not deemed an aggregation of different interests but rather as a system where each individual was expected to abide by a particular interpretation of the general will. Ethnically or religiously informed identities in particular were sidelined (Seufert, 2000). In the 1930s the principles of Kemalism were formulated. Enshrined in the constitution in 1937, these were formulated in order to define a hegemonic secular discourse that would ensure the success of the post-Ottoman nation-building process (Poulton, 1997). The secular state and its governing discourse ended up being defined through a series of binaries, such as 'progressive vs. conservative; modern vs. traditional; progress vs. backward', ultimately delineating the social and political landscape in secular vis-à-vis non-secular terms (Keyman, 1995). The essentialist nature of this language, which expresses the belief among the Kemalists that certain concepts were so important they should be taught methodically to all citizens, left virtually no room for alternative views to surface on the public agenda. Civil society became to reflect these divisions between what was to be regarded as official (secular/Kemalist) civil society and the rest of civil society.

For the masses, however, this discourse was not entirely convincing, as they were unable to sympathize with the reformist logic. The new Republic was not able to create a meaningful social agenda that resonated with the rural masses in particular (Mardin, 1995). So while the Kemalist ideas and policies enjoyed a hegemonic position in Turkish society, alternative conceptions remained alive and well in the private sphere of individuals. As Keyman has observed, the elite orientation of the reform movement meant that villages and particularly the Eastern part of the country, away from the centres of power, were much less likely to internalize the new values and norms (1995). The dominance of Kemalism in public life meant that public expressions of difference, through mediums such as civil society, were not tolerated and left civil society with very little room to grow unless attached to the official Kemalist ideology.

Political chronology: 1940s–70s

Up until 1946 the Turkish state functioned more or less as a single-party dictatorship. It was a case of 'radical change first, democracy only later' (Dodd, 1992). Atatürk in fact experimented with the idea of parliamentary democracy by arranging the founding of an opposition party – the Free Party – to his own Republican People's Party (*Cumhuriyet Halk Partisi* – CHP) in 1930. The new party was overwhelmed by membership requests, breathing life into the smouldering discontent against the single-party state and fuelling mass demonstrations. Faced with such outcome, Atatürk withdrew his support, and the party was dissolved the same year it was founded (Dodd, 1992; Weiker, 1990). In 1946, Ismet Inönü, Turkey's second president following the death of Atatürk in 1938, organized the first multiparty elections, which his party, the CHP, won comfortably. During the next four years however, the main opposition party, the Democrat's Party (*Demokrat Partisi* – DP), did their homework and were well prepared for the 1950 elections (Sunar, 2004).

In 1950, the DP won a landslide victory in the general election. The DP stood for a less militant form of secularism than the CHP, and were seen as the champions of the people with a large slice of their vote coming from the rural peasantry (Tachau and Good, 1973). The DP won convincingly again in the 1954 general election, but its gradual downfall begun in 1955. Adnan Menderes, the prime minister, had begun to assume – much like the CHP before the DP – that the government constituted the state, even denying the CHP airtime on the radio on the grounds that radio was an 'organ of the state' (Dodd, 1992, p. 20). This combined with worsening economic performance led to reduced popularity. Relations between the government and the opposition gradually deteriorated, until on 27 May 1960 the military stepped in, masterminding a coup d'état. Despite the undemocratic end to the period, the 1950s marked the emergence of civil society as an actor in Turkey's political dynamics. One sign of this was the establishment of the first labour federation, the Confederation of Turkish Trade Unions (*Türkiye İşçi Sendikaları Konfederasyonu* – TÜRK-İŞ), in 1952. The TÜRK-İŞ represented anti-communism, patriotism and non-partisanship, retaining a non-political stance wherever possible (Blind, 2007). In the 1950s society began to emerge as an 'independent entity' in Turkey (Sunar, 2004, p. 54), able to flex its muscle in support of political parties of its own choosing.

Following the 1960 coup, hundreds of DP political activists were arrested and Adnan Menderes together with two close associates were executed. In 1961, prior to the elections, the DP was outlawed. In the four years that followed, the clumsy coalition governments between the CHP and the Justice Party (*Adalet Partisi* – AP) struggled to agree on economic and domestic policy while operating under the military's watchful eye. In 1965 the AP, the political descendant of the DP, won a clear majority and was able to bring temporary stability to Turkish politics. However, the AP was soon struggling to manage the new Right–Left politics that were entering Turkey's political stage (Sunar and Sayarı, 1986). Influenced by the leftist student movements in Europe, particularly France, the youthful activists on both sides of the Right–Left continuum engaged in increasingly violent acts. In 1967, the TÜRK-İŞ stepped in to quell a strike organized by a group of factory workers and expelled the unions involved in the strike, which led to the establishment of the Revolutionary Labour Unions Confederation of Turkey[2] (*Türkiye Devrimci İşçi Sendikalari Konfederasyonu* – DİSK) that pursued a more political, independent and socialist line of action (Blind, 2007). In 1970 the more radical leftist groups carried out a systematic campaign of terrorism in order to destabilize the country (Zürcher, 2005). A wave of bombings, bank robberies and kidnappings ensued to which the nationalist groups on the right responded, soon matching the leftist movement in levels of violence. By 1971, the military establishment, convinced that the government was not able to contain the increasing violence, issued a military memorandum and on 12 March the AP-led government resigned. The 1960s in Turkey thus witnessed how civil society entered the political arena with a bang. By the early 1970s, the military had intervened and forced civil society to retreat into the trenches. From here on, the military and secularist elite regarded freely organized civil society as a potential threat to Turkey's political stability.

Between 1971 and 1980, there were two elections and ten different governments in Turkey. Three quarters of voters supported one of the two main parties, the CHP led by Bülent Ecevit, and the AP led by Süleyman Demirel. Yet it was the two right-wing fringe parties, Necmettin Erbakan's National Salvation Party (*Milli Selamet Partisi* – MSP) that supported fundamentalist Islamic principles and Arpaslan Türkeş' ultranational and pro-fascist Nationalist Action Party (*Milliyetçi Hareket Partisi* – MHP) that held the balance of power in the rickety coalition governments (Gunther, 1989). To consolidate their positions, the MHP launched the Nationalist Labour Unions' Confederation (*Milliyetçi İşçi Sendikaları Konfederasyonu* – MİSK) in 1970, to be followed in 1976 by the MSP launching its own labour federation, the Confederation of Turkish Just Workers' Union (*Hak İşçi Sendikaları Konfederasyonu* – HAK-İŞ). These unstable times witnessed a return to political violence, which escalated in the late 1970s. The youth movements at the extreme ends of the Left–Right continuum recruited new members among the discontented, unemployed youth. In January 1980, members of the DİSK clashed with military troops in Izmir, sending a ripple effect through the city, sparking several new clashes as students joined in on the fight (Gunther, 1989). The events culminated in the assassination of a former Prime Minister Nihat Erim by leftist terrorist groups, to which their right-wing counterparts responded by murdering Kemal Türkler, the former president of the DİSK. Eventually the army responded by carrying out a coup d'état on 12 September 1980. By this time society was so saturated by such tense political activity between the far left and far right forces that 20 people were killed each day due to political violence (Heper, 1985).

Year 1980 as watershed: The birth of a multi-tiered civil society

In the aftermath of the 1980 military coup, an increasing plurality of voices began gradually to find space within civil society. In an answer to the political tensions that had gripped Turkey, there was a conscious shift in focus from defending the Kemalist project from religious and ethnic divergence to actively depoliticizing society. Politically motivated civil society activity was believed to have contributed to the civil violence that preceded the coup, and action was taken to prevent the politicization of associations and unions in the future (Dodd, 1992, p. 23).

In its efforts to realign the political spectrum in a way that would destabilize the Left–Right divisions, the military junta found a useful ally in moderate Sunni Islam. The purpose of the alliance was to quell the Marxist and Fascist movements, and begin to stabilize social relations. This policy was framed as the 'Turkish–Islamic Synthesis', aiming to utilize Islam in the struggle against Kurdish nationalists and leftists in particular. To this end, the significance of Islamic values was emphasized within the official government discourse (Kadioğlu,

1996). A policy of active support was realized by encouraging the establishment of Imam Hatip Schools (Kubicek, 1999). These were vocational schools with an emphasis on religious education, and led to the establishment of several civil society associations for the purposes of their management (Grigoriadis, 2009, p. 50). By this point the Islamic movement also benefited from the efforts of a well-educated and adaptable leadership, which was able to negotiate a rhetorical path between traditional values and modernism, and thus make the most of this newfound political legitimacy (Kubicek, 1999; Yavuz, 2003). Religious intellectuals were thus able to offer an increasingly persuasive synthesis of tradition and modernism and were able to launch a more politicized campaign in its support. The emergence of political Islam as a key force in Turkish politics has been perhaps the most significant long-term outcome of the 1980 coup.

Global market forces and the logic of liberal market economics entered Turkey in the 1980s, punching holes in the insular and protective economic policies that had dominated until then. In 1980 Turkey began the implementation of a series of long-term structural neoliberal reforms under the auspices of the International Monetary Fund (IMF). Trade liberalization, privatization and a growth in exports were three of the key drivers behind the market-based reforms (Öniş and Şenses, 2007, p. 15) and by the mid-1980s Turkey had received five consecutive structural adjustment loans from the World Bank (WB) and become the number one recipient of structural funds from the IMF. Turkey was even regarded as a particularly successful example of a country that had adopted a structural adjustment programme (Keyman and Öniş, 2007, p. 107; Mosley, Harrigan and Toye, 1991, p. 9). Economic liberalization was another factor that contributed towards a more open political system where the claims made by the Kemalist elite to represent a universal ideology for the whole of Turkey was becoming increasingly unconvincing.

The 'autonomization' and 'essentialization' of civil society

The transition witnessed in the 1980s was hence one from 'confrontation to tolerance' (Göle, 1994, p. 213). Through the relative autonomization of economic activities, political groups and cultural identities, an autonomous civil society began to develop, shifting the focus increasingly from state to society. Instead of questioning or supporting the legitimacy of the ruling regime, the debate focused on particular policies. One component of this change was the rise of a new kind of 'technocratic elite' among Islamic intellectuals whose rhetoric synthesized Islamic values with the values of the modern Turkish state. In addition women, gay activists and environmentalists were successful in carving out new spaces for themselves within civil society and making louder demands on the government. What followed was not a depoliticization, argues Göle, but 'politics of different style' where people of differing political opinions would frequent the same coffeehouses and engage in debate that no longer ended in stalemate (1994, pp. 219–20).

However, despite an increasingly autonomized civil society, other elements of civil societal activity have not seen a matching change. Fuat Keyman, for example, does not think that the nature of the debate changed. Like Göle, Keyman agrees that there is now an increasing number of voices able to stake their claim through civil society, challenging the cultural homogeneity of the past. Yet he asserts that the debate is still conducted in a binary-seeking, essentialist spirit (Keyman, 2000). The emergent particular discourses should all constitute part of an array of discourses coexisting in a pluralist civil society. Instead, the Islamist discourse, for example, tends towards the formation of a new singularity, a new 'totalizing discourse' that aims to replace the universal discourse of the Kemalists with another (Keyman, 1995, p. 71). Consequently, civil society has emerged as the new battleground where the debate has retained its essentialist nature, the Kemalist and Islamic groups leading the charge.

The EU pre-accession phase

Europeanization remains an important concept in explaining social change in Turkey over the past two decades. The effect of Europeanization has been to change the context in which state–society relations are being negotiated in Turkey because such external criteria limit the ability of national political actors to maintain their hegemonic positions (Keyman and Icduygu, 2003). These outside forces have, for example, had a significant role in breaking up a previously homogenized culture, contributing in turn to the emergence of local identities (Kadioğlu, 1996). Since Turkey's membership in the Council of Europe in 1949, and later when Turkey's ambitions to accede to the EU sprang out of the starting blocks, Turkish policy has been notably influenced by the recommendations made by the EU (Karaosmanoğlu, 1994). EU civil society policy in Turkey, which was outlined in some detail in Chapter 3, can be regarded as an extension of these broader aims that seek to change the state-centred nature of Turkish politics and policymaking.

Although the Turkish case may not qualify for the classical defini-tion of Europeanization as member countries adapting to various rules and norms of the European Union, the criteria Turkey faces as a candidate country leads to virtually identical challenges. The processes of fulfilling the Copenhagen Criteria and attempting to harmonize the various chapters in the pre-accession negotiations equate with the policy and political Europeanization as described by Thomas Diez and colleagues (Diez, Agnantopoulos and Kaliber, 2005). Policy Europeanization, in a nutshell, amounts to the changes that are taking place as a result of Turkey's gradual adoption of the EU policy framework (the EU *acquis*). This consists of the one-way imposition of particular policies and political structures – spreading the European norms on policy design. Political Europeanization refers to the integration of executive and administrative structures, how to improve the efficiency and decision-making in policy, as per European standards, and ensuring that the policy reforms are successfully implemented. This view of Europeanization therefore resonates more with rational choice institutionalism and histori-cal institutionalism, which both emphasize the role and impact of European institutions in determining how domestic processes of Europeanization unfold. Potentially, these processes alter the domes-tic political and societal context of Turkey in important ways. From a civil society point of view, the adoption of European norms opens up new fields of activities, which either takes place in the expanded societal space that is made available to them, or makes use of the new policy language that has been introduced.

However, NGOs are also an object of Europeanization themselves. They are expected not only to benefit from a Europeanized social and political set-up that is more conducive to civil societal activity, but also to internalize the European norms within their own behaviour and, as such, be themselves Europeanized. Often those commenting on EU impact on civil society focus on the structural and political improvements that contribute to an environment where NGOs are more able to act. In addition, this book also asks how processes of Europeanization affect NGOs directly, how organizations respond to these processes, and in doing so reflects the sociological institutionalist approach to Europeanization.

Reform, civil society and Europeanization

The reform process in relation to EU accession, therefore, raises interesting questions about the role of civil society. Are NGOs merely following in the slipstream of an accession process directed by the EU and taking advantage of the opportunities brought about by consequences of democratic reform? Or is the role of NGOs integral to seeing through the democratic reform process successfully? It is clear that much of Turkey's reform process has been motivated by the EU, evident from the wave of policy reforms that began in the aftermath of the 1999 candidacy status: between 2001 and 2004, in a mere two and a half years, no less than nine constitutional reform packages were passed through parliament (Müftüler-Baç, 2005). Primarily, Europeanization has appeared in the form of pressures emanating from a potential EU membership upon the administrative institutions at the centre of government. This is not surprising: when Turkey became a candidate country the next logical step was to undertake wide-ranging political reforms in order to begin accession negotiations. In this sense, Europeanization has thus far been interpreted largely as democratization, and the EU incentive has been tremendously successful. This equates, more or less, to the policy and political Europeanization referred to by Diez and colleagues earlier. The debate, however, has been relatively limited to the field of high politics where civil society has played less of a role. The next challenge, Müftüler-Baç notes, is to ensure that the political reforms are actually adopted and implemented (2005). In essence, what she is referring to is societal Europeanization, internalization of the policy and political Europeanization that has so far taken place. It may be, therefore, that from the point of view of civil society actors, the real work is only about to begin.

The nature of Europeanization in the context of accession-related reform says something interesting about the role of civil society in the pre-accession process. Civil society can function as a 'pincer', for example, by influencing the processes and content of both political and policy Europeanization (Kubicek, 2005). In other words, societal

Europeanization has already taken place at least in some level, as civil society actors are advocating for further Europeanizing changes. The second issue to consider is how to get from policy and political Europeanization to societal Europeanization. Here NGOs could be involved in carrying the process of Europeanization from merely changing laws to being internalized by society at large. In equal measure NGOs may actively resist these processes and argue against further harmonization along European lines. Both sides of the debate are reflected in the domestic political arena.

What motivates domestic decision-makers such as politicians to engage in Europeanization processes? As Kubicek asks, is the reform predicated on it being appropriate (it is the right thing to do), or leading to the right consequences (it has to be done for EU membership)? He leans towards the latter, since the costs of compliance would otherwise be too high: too much ground would be yielded to minority groups without political gains (Kubicek, 2005). Such issues are underlined by the fact that the short-term costs of reform look relatively high when weighed against the long-term gains of membership, especially when one considers the uncertainty over the eventual outcome of the accession negotiations (Tocci, 2005). The commitment to the reforms is then, perhaps, somewhat erratic.

These difficult assessments have been confounded by the election results since 2002, and the reshuffling of political positions that followed. It was in 2002 that the Justice and Development Party (*Adalet ve Kalkınma Partisi* – AKP), the political party with an Islamic genealogy came to power. This has added an interesting dynamic to the whole process. Politics in the AKP era present a paradox: the political party representing the conservative and Islamic interests in society, with a tradition of opposing Europeanization, has become its strongest supporter. At the same time, the Kemalist elite, the former modernizer, has withdrawn their unreserved support for the European project. By claiming initiative on the EU agenda, the AKP has been able to anchor itself in the heartland of political centre-left, and gain votes from the liberal elite of Turkey as well as from the new middle classes benefiting from the export-oriented policies of the AKP (Pamuk, 2008; Wiltse, 2008). In its political calculus, the AKP deems the EU to be a lesser opponent than the secular establishment in Turkey, leading many secularists to remain sceptical of the zeal behind AKP's efforts at democratization. On another front, in an effort to garner populist votes, many Kemalist politicians have tapped into the nationalist backlash against the EU that has swept across Turkey in recent years. They have adopted a more critical stance on the EU, accusing it of making unreasonable demands and being disingenuous in its efforts to include Turkey. These changes in the political discourse at the top have meant that the notion of who in Turkey is being Europeanized has shifted, together with the notion of who defines or stakes a claim on what Europeanization means and where it will lead Turkey (Müftüler-Baç, 2005). In this way, EU accession process is intricately entangled in Turkey's domestic politics.

Shades of civil society in Turkey

This section aims to trace the civil societal developments since 1980 in more detail, exploring different perspectives. The first two parts consider the role of Islam and secularism in shaping civil society, and the third explores the nature of the women's movement in more detail. The final part offers examples from relations between Turkey's political culture and civil society in order to illustrate further how politics affects civil societal development in Turkey.

Islam and civil society

From the early years of the Republic until the early 1980s, Islam was deliberately confined to the outskirts of the state. The Islamist vision of a single Islamic community that would transcend nation states was promptly challenged by the vigour of Turkish nationalism (Kadioğlu, 1996). In response to this, political Islam shifted from state to society, from where it emerged as a political ideology during the times of political upheaval in the 1960s and late 1970s. Until the 1980s, the principal aim of political Islam was to resist the modernization efforts of the secular elite, recapture the state and reintroduce Islamic rule in Turkey (Yilmaz, 2007). Religiously motivated civil society groups had very little room to manoeuvre between the radicalized Islamic political agenda and the secular state determined to restrain Islamic political groups.

In the post-1980 era, however, the Islamic political agents in Turkey have changed their position. Their identity has shifted to become more accepting of modernity, rephrasing modernity in Islamic terms that offers a credible challenge to the Kemalist interpretation.

The political element of Islam is no longer categorically radicalized. The new discourse has been able to challenge the hegemony of the secular nation state while embracing the legal framework of the democratic and pluralistic parameters. This does not mean that the entire Islamic movement has shifted towards a new direction, but rather that it has become more fragmented, pulling in various directions (Yavuz, 2003). This variety reflects increasing opportunities and space for Islamic civil society activity, and has paved the way for a variety of women's group to emerge, for example. Both Yilmaz and Yavuz observe that the key challenge going forward is to find ways to expand the public sphere that make it possible to integrate the modern Muslim identities within it. Doing so is likely to reduce the social polarization that currently exists and to reduce political upheaval. CSOs are potentially a key player in any such reconciliation efforts.

The Fethullah Gülen movement is probably the most interesting example of modern Islamic thinking in Turkey. Their approach to Islam has been heavily influenced by the *Nurcu* movement, referring to those following the writings of Said Nursi (1877–1961). A prominent religious authority, Nursi's writings gained widespread popularity through Turkish society in the 1950s, despite best efforts by the state to prevent this (Aras and Caha, 2000). A key premise behind the *Nurcu* and Fethullah Gülen movements is the belief that religion and science are not irreconcilable, but rather the rationality of science and spirituality of religion complement each other (Yavuz, 1999). Neither is it necessary nor helpful to speak of a clash between the East and the West, these modern Islamic scholars assert (Aras and Caha, 2000). Democracy and Islam are not contradictory. This happy marriage between tradition and modernity resonates strongly with the views advocated by the forefather of Turkish nationalism, Ziya Gökalp. In doing so the movement is publicly subordinating itself to the dominant discourse on Turkishness that is based on nationalism and secularism, to the extent that it upholds the primacy of the nation state over individual rights. On this point of nationalist undertones the Gülen movement diverts from the mainstream *Nurcu* movement. However, by embracing a general discourse based on human rights and democracy, the Gülen movement has also been able to question the exclusivity of the Kemalist worldview in terms that cannot be ignored.

Fethullah Gülen has been spearheading a movement that encourages Muslims to become more involved in the socio-political life of Turkey without compromising their Islamic identity in order to do so. This is possible, they argue, as long as a dialogue exists between Muslim and secular elements of society. The Gülen movement is a prime example of how religiously motivated associational activity has become increasingly commonplace in Turkey, and poses a difficult hurdle for those who see increased Islamization of society as a problem.

Secularism and civil society

In the post-1980 environment, the state rhetoric of Kemalism was increasingly questioned and under pressure to adapt. The emergence of a variety of new voices within civil society exposed Kemalism as a clunky way to look at the world, particularly since the post-Cold War world no longer valued authoritarian solutions. Thus methods that had worked in 1960, 1971 and 1980 in the form of coups d'état were likely to have much more significant negative consequences after 1980. In this context, CSOs became an important vehicle for adapting Kemalism to manage the new balance of power in the 1990s and 2000s.

To illustrate the change, we can look at an example of a rhetorical shift in regard to civil society, where traditional Kemalist position has lost ground. As has already been alluded to, Turkish nationalism and Kemalism have been deemed crucial in explaining what kind of behaviour is to be regarded as civil, and thus acceptable within the realm of CSOs (Seufert, 2000). Turkish nationalism and Kemalism constituted the common denominator which appropriate civil society activism should adhere to. It was aimed to legitimate certain type of behaviour within civil society that coincided with the cultural and civilizational (in terms of Westernization and modernization) aims of the Kemalist state elite. While during the unstable 1950s, 1960s and 1970s this may have been justifiable, it was less so in the post-1980 context.

In the mid-1980s Turkey's Prime Minister Turgut Özal criticized these civilizational aims because they did not amount to a 'civilianizational' aim (Evin, 1994). This is an important terminological distinction in Turkish, for the word 'civil' (*sivil*) indicates something that is non-military.[3] In other words, when Özal was suggesting that

Turkish policy must pursue convergence between being civilized and being civilian, he meant that Turkish policymaking should no longer tiptoe around the military and prioritize society instead. At the time policy failed on this account because the military elite continued to judge civilian behaviour not on its own merits, but on the basis of how it reflects a Kemalist reading of acceptable behaviour. The statement was a direct challenge to the political role played by the military, also questioning the legitimacy of the authoritarian, or militaristic, aspects of the Kemalist position. Was the state justified in its top-down imposition of the Kemalist worldview? As the authoritarian version of Kemalism was losing its legitimacy, particularly in the face of an increasingly pluralist civil society, the Kemalist movement also began to shift in the direction of civil societal space. The emergence of Kemalist NGOs can therefore be seen as a move to rearticulate the Kemalist rhetoric in a more civilian version of itself (Erdoğan, 2000).

The events surrounding the 'postmodern coup' of 1997 help to illustrate the relationship between Kemalist civil society and the state in more detail. Coined the '28 February process', the coup originated in the unprecedented electoral success of the Islamist Welfare Party (*Refah Partisi* – RP) in the December 1996 election. During the subsequent tug-of-war between the new government on one side and the secular state elite and military on the other, the RP was ousted from power. In early 1997, on 28 February, the National Security Council (NSC) issued a statement making a series of recommendations for government policy. These included turnarounds on aspects of religious policy that had been advocated since the early 1980s, as the NSC called for restrictions in religious activism and curbs on educational establishments run by religious entities (such as Imam Hatip schools). The government refused to act upon these recommendations and was eventually forced to resign, and in January 1998 the RP was shut down and its operations deemed illegal (Karaman and Aras, 2000).

From May 1997 onwards trade unions, professional groups and women's groups – for example – joined in what became coined as the battle to save secularism and democracy as well as to protect the Turkish nation with its Atatürkian heritage (Seufert, 2000). Two leading Kemalist NGOs, the Association for Kemalist Thought (*Atatürkçü Düşünce Derneği* – ADD) and the Association for the Support of Modern Life (*Çağdaş Yaşam Destekleme Derneği* – ÇYDD), conducted joint press conferences in favour of overthrowing the RP government. Together with a number of Labour Unions they joined the 'Union of Non-Governmental Organizations' (*Sivil Toplum Kuruluşları Birliği*), signing a joint declaration against the 'anti-democratic and anti-laïc acts' of the government (Erdoğan, 2000, p. 256). What is more, the members of the NSC actively solicited this support from civil society, arranging meetings with the heads of the Kemalist NGOs. These organizations then took part in the public discussion in the media and took to the streets in protest, all in order to legitimize the anti-government position established by the NSC. This example is a pertinent illustration of how civil society participation in political debates unfolds along Gramscian lines.

Women's movement

Throughout the history of the Turkish Republic, women's issues headlined the project of modernizing and civilizing Turkey. Women's formal emancipation was achieved early as part of the legal reforms that followed the establishment of the secular republic in 1923. The adoption of a new Civil Code in 1926 made polygamy illegal and gave women equal rights to divorce and the custody of children. In 1930 women were given the right to vote in local elections and from 1934 women could vote in national elections, as well as hold public offices. These rights were not achieved through women's activism, however, but were granted by an 'enlightened governing elite committed to the goals of modernization and "Westernization"' (Kandiyoti, 1987, p. 320).

While for some these developments were inevitable steps to achieving democracy and civil society in the Turkish context, others have interpreted women's rights to have played a strategic role in destabilizing the ideological roots of the Islamic political and ideological system. Women were identified as the group most vulnerable to oppression under an Islamic regime and central to the republican struggle against the Islamic forces in Turkish society (Tekeli, 1981).

Thus, the emergent feminist movement of the 1930s was limited to issues in the public sphere that coincided with the secular state-building project. Women were perceived to have benefited from the reforms introduced by Atatürk in several ways: Western clothing for women was encouraged while the veiling of women was discouraged, and a new civil marriage was introduced banning polygamy.

Recalling the modernizing zeal of the early Republic, women were expected to embrace the new freedoms and civilized ways of being, as defined by the Republican elite. The ideal of a modern Turkish woman could therefore be summed up as married, unveiled and in public service. However, the reforms were purely focused on the public sphere, leaving patriarchal family structures of the private realm untouched (Ayata and Tütüncü, 2008; Tekeli, 1990), leaving women 'emancipated but unliberated' (Kandiyoti, 1987). Only the public element of women's rights was seen as relevant, and the embryonic feminist movement became overlapped with the secular state ideology. Gaining full voting rights as early as 1934 may in fact have been counterproductive, as this led to claims that gender equality had already been achieved. Feminism was underlined by a strict separation of state and religion as well as an aspiration for a modern republic in the image of the West. This form of 'state feminism' (White, 2003) meant that the dominant voice within the movement was focused on the public, secular role of women, leaving all other issues facing women in the private sphere outside its immediate agenda.

The development of civil society in Turkey echoes many of the ideas expressed by Ferguson, Hegel, de Tocqueville and Gramsci. Civil society in Turkey has evolved parallel to commercialization and capitalist development, where the economic liberalization efforts of the 1980s in particular were reflected in the growth of pluralist civil society. Perhaps the most pertinent observations come from Hegel and Gramsci, as Hegel described the inherent competition present in civil society and Gramsci pointed to the hegemonic versus counterhegemonic struggles that take place in civil society. These characteristics are indeed descriptive of how civil society has played out in practice. It is therefore less certain whether the donors' perception of civil society in Tocquevillean terms as a democratic counterweight to the state remains accurate in the case of Turkey.

Political culture and civil society

Civil society may be eager further to develop its voice and become a greater player in society, and forces within the EU may be keen to see civil society take a greater role; but what are the limitations to civil societal development within Turkey? This section will attempt to chart aspects of the political and social boundaries for civil societal development, for the political culture in Turkey remains antagonistic to civil societal development. Through specific examples, this section highlights the important role played by a strong state tradition in Turkish politics, and illustrates the kinds of issues that the EU civil society policy intends to address. Party structures and their policies remain hierarchical and top-down, failing to support a stronger civil society (Rubin, 2002). The political debate in Turkey tends to gravitate heavily towards issues of high politics, such as the overall nature of democracy and secularism, and the role of religion in politics, devaluing the more mundane problems of effective practical policy-making (Heper, 2002). The prominence of ideological debates in politics has led to most issues being interpreted in essentialist either/or terms. Party leaders, in the heavily hierarchical party system, become representatives of these differing worldviews and the party becomes their personal fiefdom. The arrangement lacks intra-party democracy and the space for constructive debate, leaving many socio-economic groups outside all public decision-making processes (Heper, 2002, p. 145). Civil society is notably affected by the political culture that emerges from this system.

The events surrounding the 1999 Marmara earthquake serve to illustrate these points. The earthquake impacted one of the most industrial regions of Turkey located just outside of Istanbul, claiming between 17,000 and 20,000 lives. In the aftermath of the earthquake, civil society initially mobilized in an unprecedented way, yet the organizations involved were reluctant to sustain such a high-profile role. Although this was a natural disaster, the losses could have been significantly reduced with proper precautions (World Bank, 2001). To compound the public frustrations, the state institutions – including the military – were exposed as being utterly unprepared for the emergency, taking days rather than hours to respond to the crisis (Jalali, 2002).

Civil society groups were hailed as the heroes of the quake, able to respond immediately and provide critical assistance to the victims, particularly during the first 48 hours. During the subsequent relief effort, some 40 CSOs coordinated their activities through the formation of a Civil Society Earthquake Coordination Committee, constructing and managing a city of 2000 tents (Jalali, 2002; Kubicek, 2002). The contrast between the nature of the responses and the subsequent public support for civil society-based relief initiatives carved an unprecedented opportunity for CSOs to stake their claim as an important societal voice. However, even more striking was the reluctance of CSOs to make any use of this opportunity. Despite the political capital gained by civil society activism, the organizations were unable to channel this into gains in the political arena. The network of organizations was simply too loose to transform to an effective movement. Civil society remained 'less a "society" than simply thousands of volunteers' (Kubicek, 2001, p. 40). Gradually the state took over the humanitarian operations related to the earthquake and regained control of the agenda. CSOs managing the tent cities were asked to leave, the reluctant ones being persuaded with threats to turn off water and electricity supplies (Jalali, 2002). From a civil society perspective, the events surrounding the aftermath of the earthquake suggest that civil society is still lacking the political edge that would enable it to become more than an array of activists and organizations each with their own particular agenda.

The final illustration of state–civil society relations comes from a controversial proposal for law reform that played out in 2007. Article 301 of the Turkish Penal Code has for years been at the epicentre of the freedom of speech debates in Turkey. Prior to the changes, the article stated that it was a criminal act to insult Turkishness. Given the lack of clarity as to what Turkishness meant in this context, a wide array of cases have been made against journalists and critics of the Turkish government under the auspices of Article 301. At the end of 2006, 18 professional chambers, trade unions and other CSOs got together to discuss possible changes to Article 301 (Aktar, 2007). Three of the organizations invited to take part withdrew at once, as they saw no need to make any changes to the article and another two organizations demanded that the article be scrapped altogether. The 13 remaining organizations recommended alterations to the article.[4] Following several months of negotiation, the recommendations led to minor alterations in the legal text. The proposal suggested that the word 'Turkishness' be clarified as 'having a citizenship tie to the Republic of Turkey' and the maximum prison sentence was reduced from three to two years (*Turkish Daily News*, 2007).

Bringing civil society into the 301 debate was a shrewd political move by the AKP government, utilizing civil society to its own ends. Its actions responded to EU demands on two fronts: taking action on Article 301 and allowing for greater civil society involvement in political decision-making processes, and thus addressing demands set out by the Copenhagen Criteria on two fronts at once. In addition, the government was also able to keep a clean scorecard vis-à-vis their nationalist critics – if the recommendations went too far and the situation became too volatile, the government could still retract on amending the Article, shift blame on civil society and emerge with no significant loss of political capital. Such pragmatism was also reflected in the selection of civil society representatives for the committee: business chambers and trade unions dominated the list. Their credentials as civil society representatives extended, at best, to representing the interests of workers and businesspeople in the formal economy. It may have been more appropriate to invite representatives of those individuals who have been directly affected by the law – such as journalists' associations and human rights associations.

Conclusion

The Turkish paradox, namely the simultaneous pursuit of civilizational and cultural goals that were at odds with each other, is at the heart of understanding the character of Turkish civil society. To make this synthesis work, politics were conducted in a top-down manner that firmly sidelined diverging points of view in civil society. The synthesis was never able to weld society together, however, yielding a compartmentalized society. The differences, particularly across the secular–Islamic divide, remain a defining feature of an individual's identity. This tradition continues to cast its shadow upon the way in which voices within civil society present themselves in the public sphere. Even though the number of voices has grown exponentially, the debate in civil society has retained an either/or mentality. Established structures and learnt behaviour will affect the interaction between EU policies and the development of civil society.

The Sèvres syndrome – the suspicion of Western intentions based on the treatment Turkey experienced by the Allies after the First World War – continues as a common shorthand, particularly in political punditry, for understanding elements of Turkish foreign policy. It also remains a point to consider in the current phase of EU-motivated domestic changes. To what extent is the EU agenda guiding these developments? Or is the success of political and policy Europeanization in Turkey largely dependent on the way in which the EU project is able to navigate the domestic political dynamics?

The former Europe enthusiasts – the secular elites – have begun to doubt the propriety of the EU accession project because it has been a key part of the strategy of the Islamic AKP government claiming political centre stage. More nationalist actors have recently begun rebranding pro-Europeans as agents of the West trying to harm Turkey's national integrity. It would seem that EU policies are potentially compromised by the domestic political environment, where the meaning of Europeanization began to shift since the AKP came to power in 2002. This chapter has offered an account of likely ways in which the domestic political context of Turkey may mediate the impact of Europeanization processes, and indeed, mediate the impact of EU funding to NGOs.

The challenge remains one of ensuring that the Europeanization processes continue. This challenge is particularly acute as regards democratization, as these processes should bring the different groups in Turkish civil society closer together. From a civil society point of view, the democratic developments in Turkey since 1980 have been full of both opportunities and shortcomings. An autonomous and colourful civil society has emerged, but the new forms of organization are still caught up in the either/or-styled thinking of the past. The heterogeneous and fragmented nature of Turkish civil society and subsequent weakness as a counterpoint to the state is well documented. The historical context offers a way to make sense of the opportunities and shortcomings that are found in the current phase of civil society development. Can the EU accession process work towards narrowing the gulf that exists between the secular and Islamic camps in Turkish society?

5
NGO Relationships

This chapter aims to shed light on the nature of the relationships that Turkish advocacy NGOs engage in, both with state actors and with other advocacy NGOs. The activities of such organizations tend to focus on affecting government policy, making it important to analyse the relations that exist between state actors and NGOs. The alleged capacity of NGOs to participate at the various stages of the policymaking process contributes to the view that NGOs can improve effectiveness of these processes. Additionally, the strength in numbers element of NGO advocacy is regarded as the enabling factor behind the NGO ability to influence governmental decision-making processes (Keck and Sikkink, 1998). Thus the relationships NGOs build with each other are also at the heart of advocacy work. This collaborative element of advocacy activity remains an important reason for why a link tends to be drawn between liberal democratic practices and civil society activity – why vibrant civil society is seen as a precursor to democratization, and why donors are so enthusiastic about civil society funding. These links between issues of effectiveness and processes of democratization resonate with the EU policy documents for civil society engagement discussed in Chapter 3. The analysis of NGO relationships will therefore feed back into the assumptions about the role of civil society in EU policy, with a view to reflecting on the suitability of these in the Turkish context. While developments have taken place which indicate that a vibrant, liberal-spirited civil society may be emerging, we should be wary of drawing conclusions too quickly. There is persuasive evidence to suggest that this is not a trend that manifests itself in the everyday relations between NGOs and governmental actors, nor in the relations between NGOs.

This chapter is organized into three sections. In the first section the discussion focuses on the concept of 'advocacy', what the term means in the NGO context, what kinds of NGO roles it relates to, and underlines the linkages between the advocacy NGOs and a liberal democratic understanding of state–civil society relations. The second section explores the relationships NGOs build with governmental actors in Turkey. While there has been significant progress towards cooperation in recent years thanks to improved legislation, NGO–state relations in Turkey tend to serve the purpose of legitimizing state actions. Furthermore, the fact that these relationships have not been institutionalized (there are no formal structures for such collaborative arrangements) questions the long-term viability of these relations. In the final section, the nature of the relationship between NGOs is explored, with particular emphasis on the relationship between women's NGOs. Although there are examples of collaborative projects that have led to successful outcomes, at the level of daily activities the collaborative spirit is much less evident.

Advocacy and NGOs

Advocacy in the very broadest sense is about achieving change. The word is derived from the Latin *ad vocare*, meaning 'to speak to', arguing for a particular position. It refers, in particular, to groups that argue for a particular position, or seek to influence government policy (Clark, 2010). One angle for understanding the role of advocacy NGOs vis-à-vis the state is through NGO influence on policymaking. Najam (1999) sees NGOs as policy entrepreneurs able to engage on three different levels of policymaking. First, they can aim to influence the setting of the agenda, to have a say in what issues will be taken up in policy discussions. At the second stage, NGOs can influence the development of policies by having an impact on the choices governments have to make between various policy approaches. Finally, once a policy approach has been selected, NGOs can influence the actual methods that are implemented in realization of that policy. Najam's policy entrepreneur model assumes that a broad consensus already exists between the NGO and policymakers over the direction of a given policy. The role given to NGOs is to nudge or prod the policy onto an alternative course, but never to derail it completely. In this regard the role of NGOs as advocates of change links closely with Turkey's efforts in both policy Europeanization and political Europeanization, where NGOs assist the government in achieving the required reforms. Alternatively NGOs can use the knowledge of the reforms as the means to challenge the government to deliver on the expected changes. NGOs are also an integral part of the societal Europeanization process, of internalizing the reforms and making them meaningful in the Turkish context.

The vision of NGOs as advocates feeds into two salient assumptions about what the societal role of NGOs ought to be, both of which resonate with the liberal democratic – or donor – perspectives. First comes the assumption that NGOs challenge the autonomy of the state and in doing so check state power (Mercer, 2002). Such understanding is largely informed by NGO experiences in Eastern Europe and Latin America, and supports the neoliberal view of state–NGO relations. Civil society and state are placed in an antagonistic relationship, or a zero-sum game for autonomy and legitimacy (Trägårdh, 2007). Taking its cue from writers such as Robert Putnam, a civil society that is understood to be autonomous of the state is seen as a prerequisite of democracy and in this view NGOs are central to processes of democratization. The second assumption is that advocacy NGOs are all inherently good. The focus tends to have been on the countervailing force NGOs collectively present to the state, without problematizing the nature of civil society itself (Howell and Pearce, 2001a). By being part of civil society, NGOs are all part of the democratic process and together form a bulwark against the state. In this way there is a degree of assumed homogeneity across NGOs, in that they are all meant to share this democratizing characteristic (Chandhoke, 2007). However, a more nuanced understanding of the political role of NGOs that is less dependent on such generic assumptions is required.

This chapter problematizes these assumptions. To what extent can NGOs truly challenge the state through their advocacy? Most advocacy work takes place within the narrow constraints of established policy trajectories, where the negotiation is over nuances in the policy. When NGO advocacy is focused on policy efficacy, any outcome is also very likely to help legitimize state policy. This poses a pragmatic obstacle to the depth of the democratizing impact NGOs can have. Second, NGOs are not necessarily any more democratic in nature than the state they constitute a part of. How NGOs position themselves vis-à-vis the government or the state is contingent on the ideological and political positioning of a given NGO. Their advocacy activities are informed by this ideological agreement or disagreement.

NGO–state relations

In the current condition of NGO–state relations one can observe both positive developments towards greater collaboration between government agencies and NGOs, as well as a lack of enthusiasm for greater NGO independence and involvement in the policy processes. The current relationship is thus suspended in a transition phase between a history of mutual suspicion following the crackdown on civil society activism in the early 1980s and the dramatically improved institutional and legal framework that emerged in the run-up to the start of the EU pre-accession talks. This section discusses three aspects of the relationship that NGOs have fostered with governmental actors. The first of these elaborates on the connections that exist at the level of central government; the second explores the links with municipal government; and the third looks more closely at an EU-funded project on improving relations between NGOs and the public sector.

Central government and NGOs

There have been a number of significant changes at the level of central government that at least in theory make it possible for NGOs to lobby the government more effectively. For one, there have been a number of legal reforms which benefit NGOs. In October 2004, the Associations Law was amended, lifting several restrictions that had previously curtailed civil society activism. More recently, the Foundations Law was substantially amended in February 2008. The key changes brought about by the new laws are outlined in the boxes next:

Box 5.1   Summary of the new Law on Associations

The New Law on Associations (October 2004)

- Lifting the requirement:
  - o to seek permission when opening branches abroad, joining foreign bodies and holding meetings with foreigners
  - o to inform local officials of general assembly meetings taking place
  - o to seek permission to receive funds from abroad
- Requiring:
  - o governors to issue a warning prior to taking legal action against CSOs
  - o security forces to obtain a court order before being allowed on the premises of a CSO
- Enabling CSOs to:
  - o establish temporary platforms or networks
  - o conduct joint projects
  - o receive financial support from other associations and public institutions
- Setting up a Department of Associations within the Ministry of Interior, thus removing security forces as the first point of contact and oversight for civil society

Source: European Commission (2004b), TUSEV (2004b).

Box 5.2   Summary of the new Law on Foundations

The New Law on Foundations (February 2008)

- Tax exemptions:
  - o All foundations with or without Public Benefit status will be exempt from gift and inheritance tax; all persons making grants or expenses to foundations will be exempt from income and corporate tax
- Board membership:
  - o Removing a board member will only be possible against evidence of criminal acts

- Role of foreigners:
  - Foreigners are now able to establish foundations, and to serve as board members of existing foundations
- Foreign funding:
  - Receipt of foreign funding no longer requires a permission; a prior notification of authorities by the foundation will suffice

Source: TUSEV (2008).

The impact of these legal changes has been significant. The notion of freedom of association is no longer an oxymoron: CSOs are able to freely cooperate with other organizations, both local and foreign; they can receive funds from both local and foreign organizations without requiring government permission to do so. The two campaigns by women's groups, for example, to lobby for specific changes to the Civil and Penal Codes benefited from this changing attitude towards civil societal activity (see the third section of this chapter). The consequences of the relaxed legal framework reach beyond the technical changes to the law. It amounts to an expression of trust in these organizations – they do not need to be subject to surveillance, their operations are not clandestine or suspicious. During field research the NGO respondents offered these same two broad positive messages when asked about the positive impact of the reformed Associations Law. Non-governmental activism is no longer understood as anti-governmental.

The commissions that were set up as part of the law reform process have also opened their doors to NGOs. The law reform process requires the relevant department of the judiciary to create a commission to review the proposed reform.[1] These commissions are composed of judges, academics, representatives of NGOs and other experts on the given area of legislation. In order for an NGO to participate, first it is required to submit a written report on the subject of the reform. This is taken as an indication of their expertise on the subject, which is then reviewed by the judiciary. Since not many NGOs are able to write such reports, this in itself filters the number of organizations able to take on a committee membership down to the most capable and well resourced. However, the submission of such a report is no guarantee of participation in the commission. Representation is by invitation only, and given the limited size of these commissions, the larger and the better known NGOs tend to gain the positions within these commissions by virtue of being known to the selection committee. This also means that only a very small number of NGOs can participate in any given commission.[2]

Several NGO respondents were somewhat disillusioned by the process. Writing such reports was time-consuming work with no guarantees of a fruitful outcome. Without an invitation to participate, it was difficult to know if the recommendations of the report were in any way considered by the committee. Furthermore, what kind of report will gain an NGO the required access to the negotiating table? How critical can an NGO be of the proposed legal reform and still be successful in participating? These commissions provide NGOs with access to the negotiating table and with the chance to express their argument in favour of a certain policy direction. At the same time the top-down and hierarchical nature of the selection process for participating in committees means that this avenue is only available for a select few NGOs.

The establishment of the Department of Associations (DoA) further exemplifies the extent of the changes that have taken place in recent years. Prior to the DoA, CSOs dealt with the local police as the first point of contact on all bureaucratic matters. As respondents with personal experience recounted, it was the local police station that issued permissions to carry out projects, apply for funding and travel abroad. The issue is not only the fact that this role was given to the police, but also that standard organizational processes required official permits. The amended Associations Law, by establishing a DoA, addressed this rather uncivilian way of treating civil society and illustrates the notable extent to which the governance of NGOs has changed.

The DoA retains an aloof approach to facilitating NGO–government relationships.[3] Their point of view iterates that the reformed legal framework provides sufficient guidelines for NGOs to both lobby government and to partake in policymaking. The strategy put forward by the DoA places the onus for greater collaboration largely on the shoulders of NGOs. While government ministries are encouraged to sponsor NGO projects, there is an underlying belief that NGOs should first prove themselves to be developed enough to make good project partners. Article 10 of the new Associations Law allows ministries to co-sponsor up to 50 per cent of any NGO project. This arrangement may complement EU project funding, which expects beneficiary NGOs to find at least 10 per cent of the funds from other sources. Where such complementarity exists between, for example, the aims of the Ministry of Education and an EU project on encouraging rural families to send girls to school carried out by a youth NGO, the facility now exists to utilize such synergies. The DoA has been trying to encourage this kind of greater cooperation between NGOs and government ministries, and to this end the DoA issued a circular to all ministries to make sure that everyone is aware of the possibility for cooperation. The remaining challenge is to convince government officials that partnerships with NGOs are worth their while.

Thus far, despite wider awareness of the existence of such possibilities, there has not been a great deal of enthusiasm for such activity within the ministries. The DoA hopes that by engaging with NGOs the government can lead by example and show that these organizations are trustworthy partners, encouraging in turn the public to trust NGOs. They are not yet fully conversant with the new legislative infrastructure and are therefore not aware of all the avenues that will lead them to effective lobbying and be part of policymaking. NGOs are just beginning to emerge as a sector, and therefore need time to establish themselves within society:

> We are dealing with people that are just now forming NGOs. You must therefore be patient, more tolerant and continue to promote the [third] sector. It is important to promote trust between government and the [third] sector, and to build trust between NGOs and the public. The department [of Associations] is using the instruments it has to help, and it also makes sure the right of association is not being misused which would give the sector a bad name among public. The problem with government is that people there don't think it's worth dealing with NGOs. Here the department [of Associations] should lead by example and build confidence and trust.[4]

The previous account reveals certain assumptions about NGOs and civil society in the DoA. Basing ideas about civil society on something that is new and emerging in Turkey reveals a particular understanding of how NGOs are perceived. This understanding resonates well with words such as modern and professional, and less well with words like traditional and voluntary, in the end favouring those organizations that aspire to this particular model. Furthermore, preoccupation with projects where government agencies partner with NGOs communicates a particular understanding of what NGOs are – organizations that focus on delivering services. The way potential relationships between NGOs and government institutions are structured leave little room for NGOs to influence government policy. They can only support it.

Overall the framework for civil society participation at the governmental level is structured largely in a top-down fashion. The responsibility to develop the sector is seen to lie with NGOs and other civil society actors. While avenues exist for NGOs to participate (such as the commissions and part-funded projects), there is little room for unsolicited input and in practice the access is likely to be limited to the most capable and professional NGOs. Much more work needs to be done to ensure that institutional mechanisms are put in place that make it clear how collaboration between government ministries and NGOs should be formulated.[5] For the moment, any such cooperation is contingent on the enthusiasm that officials employed by the ministry show towards NGO involvement. Perhaps it is unrealistic to expect a more flexible arrangement at the highest levels of government. If this is the case, then relations at the municipal level may provide greater insights.

Structure of local government

Local government in Turkey is made of three entities: the provincial administration, municipal administration and the village level (Köker, 1995, p. 58; Polatoğlu, 2000, p. 157). The appointment of each governor (*vali*), the head of provincial administration, is approved by the president. Each province consists of roughly eight districts, and each district is governed by a district chief (*kaymakam*), also appointed by the president following a nomination made by the Ministry of the Interior. Municipal administration is similarly found in each provincial and district capital, as well as in any community with more than 2000 inhabitants. Each municipality is headed by a mayor who has been elected by the local citizens for a five-year term. In villages with fewer than 2000 inhabitants an assembly of village adults elect a village headman (*muhtar*) to oversee local affairs. The coexistence of two systems, based on one side on the appointments by central government, and on local elections on the other, complicates the political relationships at the local level. This is particularly true in instances where the governor's office and municipal government are represented by two different political parties. The local government actors – whether representing the governor's office or the municipal government – are not neutral and value-free in their actions. This is also likely to have an impact on how they choose to engage with the processes of policy implementation as they relate to NGO–local government relations in the context of EU-funded projects.

Local government reform has indeed also been in the agenda of EU support from Turkey. In 2004 a Local Administration Reform Programme was launched, which aimed to strengthen the capacity for local administration reform at the level of central and local government, improve financial and budgetary procedures, and develop the efficiency and effectiveness of human resource management (Ministry of the Interior, 2010). This reform programme is part of the modernization efforts that are expected to precede any future EU membership, not least because of the importance the EU attaches to local authorities. The proximity of local government to the public gives it an important role in persuading the public of the benefits of integration (Kösecik and Sağbas, 2004, p. 362).

NGO–local government relations

At the level of local government, the relations with NGOs are different because a more intimate relationship can be developed. The leadership of a municipal government is naturally a more accurate reflection of the local nuances and therefore more representative of, and attentive to, local needs and demands. However, at the same time, local government can be an unpredictable and even mercurial partner for NGOs. These relationships can pan out in a variety of ways depending on the nature of the particular local government actors the NGO is dealing with. Political affiliations and personal relationships become increasingly salient factors. The section offers examples of this diversity of ways in which these relationships develop.

The relations depict a persuasive correlation between the political alignments between local government and NGOs, and the extent of their collaboration. For example, an Islamic women's NGO interviewed in Istanbul, has developed a positive, constructive relationship with its municipal government that dates back to 1994. The municipality also happens to be governed by an Islamic party, and despite political upheaval at the national level during this time, the municipality has been consistently governed by the same party. The NGO has gradually forged a close relationship, and collaborated on a number of small-scale projects. Several of the NGO volunteers are in fact workers from the municipal government. Similarly, an Islamic women's umbrella group has also been given rent-free office space by the same municipality.[6] These relationships were built on the basis of a worldview that shared a common base in religion. Religion in the public domain, as Chapter 4 has illustrated, is virtually always a political issue. Through other interviews, I heard of other examples where political views shaped the relationship between municipal government and NGOs. A municipality in Istanbul governed by the Democratic People's Party (*Demokratik Halk Partisi* – DEHAP)[7] was unable to find a partner NGO for a project because all NGOs which were approached refused to work with the party for political reasons. In response, the municipality displayed its innovative capabilities and created its own NGO in order to qualify for the funding. In slightly different ways each of these cases illustrates the importance of congruence in political views between local government and NGOs, both as a bridge and an obstacle to collaboration.

Political alliances also played a role in determining government–NGO relationships elsewhere in the country. During the interviews I conducted in the southeast of Turkey, in Diyarbakir, every NGO I interviewed made the same distinction when asked about collaboration with government offices. They would collaborate with the municipal office, but not with the governor's office, as the latter has a tendency to treat NGOs with suspicion and refuses to participate.[8] The reasons for these differences were the following. The governor is appointed by the national government, and acts in accordance with the official government line, and can therefore be less attuned to local issues. The previous governor was more moderate in his views while the current one tends to see NGOs as an extension of the irredentist Kurdish movement. The municipal government, on the other hand, is elected locally so office-holders are more likely to be concerned with local issues and therefore also work on collaborative events with local NGOs. In this way, different sectors of government are likely to develop different kinds of relations with NGOs. One women's NGO that I interviewed in Diyarbakir described itself rather openly as a part of the municipal government. The NGO was effectively set up by the municipality in order to respond to EU calls for proposals that required local government–NGO partnerships.[9] In some of the interviews, similar anecdotal examples were repeated; often funds from the EU require cooperation between NGOs and municipalities, and in some instances this has encouraged municipalities to set up their own NGOs. These examples attest to the inventive ways that local actors have to establish NGO–local government relationship in order to qualify for EU funding (this issue of agency is taken up as one of the central themes of Chapter 7).

The lax boundaries between civil society and local government seen in the earlier example of the women's NGO that was set up by the municipality demonstrate the unorthodox way in which citizens may position themselves in relation to municipal government. Given the hostile response of the current governor towards both NGOs and the local municipal administration, it may not be as surprising that NGOs and the municipality view themselves as being on the same side, vis-à-vis the governor.

This is not to say that collaboration between NGOs and local government is not witness to any contestation. A women's NGO which runs two shelters for women suffering from domestic violence in Istanbul has collaborated with local government offices in an Istanbul municipality. Upon completion of the project, against the wishes of the NGO, the municipality insisted that the development should not be called a 'shelter'; it should instead be named 'guest-house' (*konukevi*). Using the word shelter would insinuate that there is a problem in the neighbourhood, and for this reason a guesthouse was deemed a more appropriate and neutral term to use.[10] Thus, there is a danger for the politics surrounding the projects to take over, changing the way the outcomes of a project will play out.

Similarly, in both Ankara and Istanbul the governor's office has initiated court proceedings in an effort to close gay-rights NGOs. In Istanbul, the governor's office in early 2007 filed a case against *Lambda*, the largest queer advocacy NGO in Turkey, on the grounds that its activities are 'against the law and morality of Turkey', and that the NGO's objectives were offensive to Turkish moral values and family structures (Human Rights Watch, 2008). The Ankara governor's office has also previously attempted to close down two other queer organizations, KAOS-GL and Pink Life (*Pembe Hayat*) on similar charges, but in these cases the charges were dropped by the prosecution. In November 2008, following an appeal, the proceedings against Lambda have also been dropped. Nevertheless the episode shows how local government institutions may take an interest in controlling what kind of associationalism should be allowed.

Facilitating NGO–local government relations through EU projects

As a final example of NGO–local government relations I look at an EU-funded project that aimed to facilitate the development of such connections. As has already been mentioned, in the context of the pre-accession process EU has gradually shifted its attention away from NGOs and towards a variety of governmental agents. In connection with this shift, an EU-funded pilot project was conceived that would encourage improved NGO relations with public sector agents, and with municipal governments in particular. The account presented here is looking at the project from the point of view of a children's NGO that took part in the pilot project.

The programme was set up for an initial time frame of two years, with the EU Secretary General, the Central Finance and Contracts Unit (CFCU), the British Council and the EU Delegation to Turkey as the supporting partners. In total, €2 million were committed to the programme aimed towards 'fostering cooperation and dialogue' between NGOs and the public sector (European Commission, 2007b). The project was perceived as the beginning of a long-term process of increasingly close cooperation between NGOs and municipal officials.[11] The programme had two central elements. First the programme arranged for a wide consultation process where representatives from both sides came together to produce a memorandum of understanding. This document aimed to lay out the basic principles of cooperation between CSOs and public institutions. Secondly, the programme cultivated 11 pilot projects where NGOs and public bodies acted as partners on specific projects.

So how did this project play out in practice? Here is an account from the point of view of one of the 11 NGOs that described its experience of partaking in a pilot programme.[12] In the experience of the director, the entire project was a 'disaster'. She claimed that the programme director – who had previously been employed by the CFCU – behaved like a 'military commander' and managed the operation through a series of financial threats. The NGO director was said to have frequently arrived at the office to find emails making demands such as 'the money will not be transferred to you unless you do this; unless you agree to do things our way, you will have to pay a penalty.'[13] This style of management was demotivating for the group, the NGO director recalled. She felt that the programme director did not appreciate the NGO's limited capacity to comply with such demands, especially at short notice. Managing the relationship with this intermediary organization ate up most of the productive time for the NGO. The NGO was eventually compelled to write a letter of complaint about the programme administration, copying the letter to all project partners: the EU Delegation, British Council and the EU Secretary General. Overall, the NGO was given €38,000 under the programme, but due to lack of compliance with the procedural demands for EU funding (the NGO was accused of spending the funds in what were deemed unaccountable ways), they were required to reimburse €25,000. Following long discussions with the CFCU and the EU Delegation, the amount to be reimbursed was reduced to €300. The NGO director found the whole process so draining that she made a decision not to apply for any EU funding for at least two years.

Aside from the difficulties in managing relations with the intermediary organization, the relationship with the municipal government also proved tricky and politicized. Throughout the project, the NGO had only one point of contact within the municipality. In other words, the project was not institutionalized within the municipal office. The project itself focused on working with children who had spent time at correctional institutions, with a view to facilitating their reintegration in society. This issue is central to the day-to-day work of the NGO, so the content of the project was not new to them: only the partnering organization was new. The CHP governed the municipality at the time, which is a party with a conservative policy orientation. As it happened, the project coincided with a vote in France (October 2006) on the issue of the Armenian genocide by the Ottoman armies in 1915. The vote would make it illegal to claim it was not a genocide, much like the case of the Holocaust.

Given that on issues such as this the CHP has a staunchly nationalist political stance, and refuses to recognize the events of 1915 as
genocide, the party remained adamantly against any such legislation and was actively involved in arranging protest demonstrations
outside the French embassy in Ankara. The Cankaya municipality, being governed by the CHP, also contributed to the protests.
The person at the municipal government responsible for the NGO
project on children's rehabilitation collected several of the project's
participants – children aged six to 14 – and transported them to the
demonstration. Here the children were given anti-French slogans to
carry and asked to participate in the demonstration. The project was
thus hijacked by the political processes that the municipal government was engaged in, making use of the NGO and the child beneficiaries as pawns in the political manoeuvres being executed.

This project was unable to deliver on its aims. Following the
12-month pilot programme, it was discontinued. It was difficult to
determine the reasons for this, as the informants interviewed were
unforthcoming when asked this question. The example of one of
the pilot projects described before may offer some insights, however.
For the municipality to assign one member of staff to work on the
project does not suggest that the project was seen as the beginning of
a long-term partnership, nor did it reflect a change in how relations
with NGOs were operationalized. If that member of staff had been
more dynamic and interested in the project and the work the NGO
was doing, the project may well have been much more successful.
Having just one point of contact within the municipality did mean
that the project lacked institutionalization, but this, as long as the
right people are involved, does not necessarily mean that the project
will necessarily be a failure. What it does suggest, however, is that
the transaction costs for participating in such projects tend to be too
high for governmental actors to truly engage in them.[14] The costs in
terms of time and political ability outweigh the benefits of genuine,
full participation.

This may also tell us something about the limits of what can
be achieved through project-based development. The project was
conceptualized between the EU Delegation, the CFCU and the EU
Secretary General, and €2 million were introduced into the equation.
The only common denominator between the municipality and the
NGO was the project and the funding. There may have been a valid

reason why these two actors would not have worked together under normal circumstances – perhaps their political views were too different, a reason that was suggested earlier. Partnership for the sake of partnership may not be that constructive.

Exposing the different layers of relations between NGOs and representatives of the state reveals a variety of relationships. While the opportunities for engagement are much narrower at the level of central government, here the channels have been more institutionalized than at the level of municipal government. NGO relations with municipal government vary, largely because municipalities represent a spectrum of political positions in a way that central government does not. Although there are more possibilities for NGO–government relationships at the local level, these are not as well established as those at the central government level and have the potential to play out in a variety of ways. Beyond this NGOs can of course enhance their voice by gaining the support of the broader public, or indeed by working together with other NGOs.

NGO–NGO relations

If relationships with governmental entities offer only limited opportunities for engagement, then good relations with other NGOs can offer greater scope for NGOs to influence government policy. This section explores this claim by looking at examples from within the women's movement in Turkey. Women's groups in Turkey make for an interesting case because while a broad array of women's NGOs have collaborated successfully in policy campaigns, there are deep-seated sources of tension within the movement as well. The case presents both opportunities and shortcomings for advocacy activities in Turkey and suggests that civil society is still going through growing pains. As a result, it does not necessarily contribute to democratization in the way that EU policy anticipates. Given the essentialist tendencies of NGOs in Turkey, what remains unresolved is the question of how to allow all points of view to be given space, while also ensuring appropriate guidelines for tolerance and cooperation.

Successful NGO relationships between women's NGOs

During the last decade the women's movement in Turkey has had a significant impact on the reform process that has paved the road to greater gender equality. Although the realization of these reforms was set as a precondition for the beginning of the EU accession process, the women's movement has nevertheless played a significant role in shaping the final mould of these reforms. The new Turkish Civil Code, adopted in 2001 integrated many of the amendments women's NGOs had advocated for since the early 1980s. It abolished the position of a man as the (legally recognized) head of the family and provided women with new legal rights in marriage and divorce. Spurred on by the success of the campaign to reform the civil code, the women's movement regrouped behind another campaign to reform the Turkish Penal Code (Anıl et al., 2005). Following three years of campaigning, a new Penal Code was adopted in 2004, representing another major shift in gender equality. Sexual violence is now regarded as a crime against the individual, not against society; rape within marriage now constitutes a crime; and a rapist can no longer marry their victim as a means to avoid punishment. In all, over 30 recommendations made by the campaign were included in the final document (Anıl et al., 2005). In these two cases women's NGOs have been tremendously successful in influencing legal reform – or legal Europeanization – in the context of the EU reform process.

Although the reform process has provided a focus around which women's activism could crystallize in recent years, it is important to consider the role played by women's NGOs in the context of the wider story of women's activism. As Chapter 4 has already outlined in more detail, the current women's movement in Turkey dates back to the 1930s, to the early years of the republic, when women's liberation became a symbol for the kind of modernization and progress the new leadership aspired to. As such, it was juxtaposed against the Islamic tradition that represented a traditional and backward role for women. For a long time it was the secular, modern women – the state feminists as they were described in Chapter 4 – who occupied the civil societal space (Tekeli, 1981). Particularly since 1980, following the military coup, a more diverse set of organizations has gradually come to inhabit women's civil society. The impact of this has been most visible in the growth of the Islamic women's movement since the late 1980s (Göle, 1994); and the bipolarity of women's civil society, poised between the secularist and Islamic influences (Keyman, 1995), has become increasingly clear.

It is therefore somewhat surprising that despite the increasing polarity within the women's movement, NGOs across the spectrum came together behind the campaigns on legal reform. How should we explain this success of the women's NGOs in influencing the legal reform process? When I put this question to the respondents, they pointed at three possible explanations.[15] First was the urgency of the issue. The parliamentary discussions regarding the Penal and Civil Codes took place over a limited time frame, after which the window of opportunity to have an impact would pass. The awareness among women's groups that success would require a short, high-impact campaign brought many of them together for the first time. The second factor was the universal nature of the issues that the women were demanding, which made it relatively easy for all to agree on the demands of the campaigns. In addition, these demands were not developed simply for the sake of this campaign; they had existed for a long time and had been internalized within the movement. Finally, the campaign operations were directed by a relatively small number of women. The campaign on the Penal Code, for example, was headed by members of 26 organizations (Anıl et al., 2005). This meant there were fewer differences to reconcile between the most active participants, while others were happier to follow in their slipstream. Ideological and political differences between the participants – particularly those relating to the role of religion in public life – were cast aside for the purpose of achieving lasting structural change. These are the key reasons as to why the women's NGOs were able to foster such an effective network of relationships behind a single-issue campaign.

The two campaigns paint an ideal picture of an advocacy campaign. The women's NGOs are 'prodding the government to do the right thing' as Jenkins' definition of advocacy suggests. By setting out a list of demands for legal reform, the organizations publicly challenged the state to change its ways (Tully, 2002). The campaigns were based on an antagonistic relationship with the government, making it attractive to draw comparisons with the Turkish case and the liberal democratic discourse depicting civil society as a bulwark against the state. We see an independent and well-organized movement that has been able to successfully challenge the hegemony of the Turkish state. Yet the factors contributing to the success of the Penal and Civil Code campaign suggest that these campaigns were conducted under exceptional circumstances that may not reflect the true state of the civil society in Turkey.

As these campaigns were elite-led by a small number of urban NGOs, it is important not to extrapolate overoptimistic conclusions about the state of Turkish civil society more broadly. Caution is particularly important where there are possible policy implications. The interview respondents, both civil society activists as well as EU and Turkish officials, often referred to the success of the women's movement as an example of the potential within Turkish civil society to develop. It would be tempting to conclude that women's activism offers an example of how to achieve further democratization by building a vibrant civil society. The examples here have shown there exists a group of NGOs and activists that is extremely productive, vocal and relatively influential in its criticism and commentary on government policy. At the same time, it is important to be clear of the extent to which these campaigns were a unique example of a particular, non-replicable process. As one respondent described this situation:

> There are many more opportunities to 'shake hands' for NGOs in Ankara and Istanbul. This is where the politicians are. This is where the embassies are. Also, there are people here that can help us make something with these chances, like our board members. These types of chances don't exist for organizations in Van [a city in the southeast of Turkey].[16]

Such policy influence as was evident in these campaigns can only be realized by large, professional organizations working near the central government. Another respondent remarked that in the months that followed the approval of the penal code the 'intellectual women of the movement took the message to other women, in order to inform them of their new rights and responsibilities'.[17] Although this is also an example of downward advocacy and is in itself a positive step, it should also remind us that the successes described were largely limited to the organizational elite among the women's movement. The aim is not to devalue the successes but to recognize the context in which they have been achieved, as this is important in understanding how the changing relationship between state and certain groups can (or cannot) be seen to have broader implications on state–civil society relations and democratization. It is unlikely that a similar feat of influencing government policy could be replicated in, for example, a more rural setting in Turkey, with local government and local NGOs. Here the elite NGOs were able make use of certain channels to influence government policy, who made good use of a rare window of opportunity to have a say in legal reform.

Complicated NGO relationships between women's NGOs

Shifting the focus away from the two particular legal reform campaigns, this section focuses on the more complex and colourful array of relationships that underline relations between women's NGOs. Outside the realm of the highly focused campaigns, women's NGOs have not found it very easy to collaborate. This is due to a combination of reasons that gravitate around two issues: struggles for position and ownership within the women's movements on one side, and divisions based on ideological differences on the other.

Struggles for position and ownership within the women's movement get in the way of collaboration. In 2006 the Nordic embassies in Turkey extended their support to one women's NGO by funding a campaign titled 'Women's Agenda'. The campaign was headed by a well-known women's NGO based in Ankara. Other NGOs and women activists, however, questioned the term 'women's agenda'. It was not deemed appropriate to generalize in this way when the agenda in question is a particular one devised by the organization in charge of the project. They argued that not all NGOs would agree with its content and therefore one should not regard it as an agenda for all women. In addition, others regarded the foreign funding behind the project as a problematic issue. Since it is difficult for many NGOs to access foreign funds, these kinds of funds therefore tend to gravitate towards the larger, more established organizations. 'How can such a top-down campaign be framed in terms of all women?' they questioned.[18] In other words, there is resistance to individual organizations using the collective identity of the women's movement to further their own cause.

In a similar fashion, the second example recalls the experiences of one activist attending an annual conference that was organized by a pioneering women's organization in Turkey. The conference was initially named after the organization that organized the event. A discussion took place early on among the participants whereby it was agreed

that the name should be changed, so that it would be more representative of the movement as a whole. Year after year, the name of the
conference remained unchanged, however, and continued to carry
the name of the host organization. As the respondent recalled, questions began to be raised among the participants as to who really was
claiming ownership over the conference – the participants or the host
organization.[19] This resistance towards the name of the conference
and the subsequent debate expresses the political nature of relationships within the women's movement. Like in the previous example,
other groups reacted in this way because the name of one organization was used to represent the whole of the women's movement. The
conference was understood as an attempt by one organization to
further its own agenda in the slipstream of the women's movement as
a whole. Although such political struggles are by no means unique to
Turkey or to the women's movement, it remains an issue to be borne
in mind when formulating policy.

Divisions of an ideological nature also contribute to the struggles
that occur between women's NGOs. The first of four examples illustrating this relates to the relations between Kemalist and Kurdish
NGOs taking part in the Annual Nationwide Women's Conference.
In 2005, a more explicit conflict of interests surfaced between two
camps of NGOs. One respondent described how a group of Kurdish
women's NGOs wanted to organize a breakout session to discuss
state violence against women. The secular, Kemalist NGOs refused
to allow this meeting to take place, and even called the police in an
effort to stop the breakout session from taking place. The breakout
meeting did still go ahead, but according to the respondent, the
actual purpose and aims of the conference were sidelined. The conference no longer remained a constructive platform for discussing
women's status in Turkish society as the focus had shifted onto the
internal divisions within the movement. This example also illustrates
how some Kemalist NGOs view their role as guardians of the secular
state, embracing a similar role to certain NGOs in the run-up to the
28 February Process and the postmodern coup in 1997 (as discussed
in Chapter 4).

The ideological differences between the Islamist and secular
women's NGOs are at the heart of these kinds of divisions. The
legal reform campaign referred to earlier in this chapter offers an
example of how the ideological divisions play out in practice. Yahoo!

groups – an online discussion group – became an important tool in the early phases of the campaign. The vice-president of an Islamic women's organization took part in these discussions, and her suggestions were warmly welcomed by the group of online activists. However, in these discussions it was impossible to tell that she was wearing a headscarf. Her choice to wear a headscarf became a source of contention later on during the face-to-face meetings that followed. Here the differences between secular and Islamic ideological positions took over the agenda from the issues of penal code reform, and the working relationship between the activists became more difficult to manage. These differences kept resurfacing as the campaign matured and the participating Islamic NGOs elected to opt out from supporting certain clauses in the reforms. In particular, they opposed the demand to remove all references to morality, chastity and honour from the new penal code. Additionally, the Islamic groups decided to opt out from lobbying on other issues where the reforms demanded by the campaign would have objected with their religious worldview. For them, religious commitments came first.[20] Despite the overall success of the campaign, the ideological differences among women's NGOs are of such nature that it was difficult to reconcile these in one unified campaign. These boundaries are difficult to overcome and the different priorities that exist between secular and Islamic groups are difficult to reconcile.

These ideological differences surface on various occasions. In early 2008 the new deputy director of the EU Delegation to Turkey invited 12 representatives of women's NGOs to attend a meeting at his office. According to a respondent he was very welcoming and wished to learn about the kinds of problems that women's NGOs faced with EU funding. A representative from an Islamic women's NGO, however, moved away from this topic, and insisted on questioning the official over the reasons why the EU has not been more explicit in its support for a greater freedom to wear the headscarf in Turkey. Her actions decidedly undermined the meeting, effectively derailing the discussion on the problems women's NGOs face with regards to EU funds. In other instances the ideological cleavages between secular and Islamic NGOs have undermined an entire campaign and demonstrate the tendency by NGOs to appropriate the civil societal space for particular ideological agendas. In the spring of 2008 women's NGOs planned to organize a campaign around a new issue: a government proposal for reforming the social security in Turkey. The campaign was initiated as NGOs realised that the government proposals failed to address issues of gender equality. Under the proposed reforms, women still would not have gained equal benefits. A new campaign was organized, one which bore great resemblance to the Penal Code and Civil Code campaigns mentioned earlier, with the aim of bringing these thoughts to the attention of the government and the public. However, this time fundamental divisions among NGOs were exposed by the campaign rhetoric. Public protests, in particular the overarching message delivered by these demonstrations, became a divisive issue. The comment made a member of an Islamic NGO lucidly illustrates this:

> I personally wanted to attend some street protests about this reform, but they are shouting things like 'this AKP government and this parliament are backward'. They are swearing at them because they are Muslim. I really feel that this is my problem, but I cannot attend these protests. They are swearing at us, so we cannot be together.[21]

The campaign was framed simultaneously as both promoting women's rights and protesting against the current government. The inadequacies of the reform agenda from a gender perspective were taken as evidence that the government adhered to a more conservatively religious understanding of social relations that was detrimental to further progress of women's rights. The lobbying efforts within the campaign were framed less in terms of universal women's rights and more in terms of a particular political agenda aimed at undermining the government. In this example, the secular face of the women's movement claimed centre stage within the campaign, defining it on the basis of a particular ideology and utilizing the women's movement to legitimize this position.

Conclusion

If we see NGO advocacy as a process aspiring for change then relations with governmental actors and with other NGOs are clearly important aspects of this process. Interpreting advocacy in this way in fact resonates well with the idea of Europeanization, or policy harmonization in the context of EU accession that has been discussed elsewhere in this book: Europeanization and the EU pre-accession process are both premised on change. It is therefore useful to reflect on the character of these relationships and how this relates back to EU civil society policy in Turkey.

The legal and structural reforms have contributed to the development of a more enabling environment when it comes to NGO–government relations. The process of legal reform – one of the prerequisites of the EU accession process – has set these relationships on a more formal footing. The avenues through which NGOs can influence government policy have become more formalized, and in the shape of the DoA civil society has gained a governmental actor that can facilitate this relationship. At the level of municipal government, there is a great deal of variety in how local government actors approach civil society, and how this plays out in NGO–government relations is contingent on the adaptability of the political positions each side holds. The variety of political influences that affect the character of local government means that different municipalities will offer their support to different kinds of NGOs on the basis of political affinity. Thus secular, Islamic or Kurdish NGOs can all identify access points at the level of local government.

There is, however, scope for developing these relations further. For example, the avenue for NGOs to contribute to legal reform processes remains narrow. Government departments, despite the existence of a facility where each department can co-sponsor NGO-run projects, remain reluctant to do so. At the level of local government the diversity of political opinions has proven to be a double-edged sword, as this can contribute to a political backlash against NGOs whose political ideas do not conflate with those of local government. It seems there are distinct political limitations to how far NGO–local government relations can develop at the moment. One persuasive explanatory factor can be found in the higher transaction costs that governmental actors face. In other words, NGO partnerships need to deliver politically worthwhile outcomes before governmental actors truly want to engage with NGOs.

Likewise, relations between NGOs exhibit both opportunities and shortcomings. The examples from the women's movement show that NGOs do have the potential, under the right circumstances, to successfully influence government policymaking at the highest level.

The question is, however, to what extent are the experiences of the Penal Code and Civil Code campaigns replicable elsewhere within civil society activity? Among women's NGOs, at least, opportunities for collaboration have been decidedly limited by two factors. Competition for position on one side and ideological differences on the other have both contributed to the lack of progress in reconciling the dissonances within the movement. These dynamics agree with a Gramscian reading of the situation: a struggle between hegemonic and counterhegemonic voices is being played within the women's movement.

Given the existence of competitive relationships within civil society, and the essentialist nature of the debate between the various voices within civil society, is there any scope for a successful strategy as far as the accession process goes? Somewhat counter-intuitively, the undemocratic rhetoric that emerges is an important phase in the democratizing process. The schisms between NGOs originate from important societal debates that should not be ignored and which need to be sustained. One could regard them as growing pains in the context of democratization. In this context, the long-term goal of the accession process should be the determination of common denominators for public debate that guarantee freedom of expression. This should contain parameters that ensure tolerance prevails in the heated and important debates that take place.

6
Civil Society Support in Turkey

The purpose of this chapter is to draw a picture of the funding environment for civil society in Turkey, and describe the way NGOs behave in this environment. The aim is to understand how the availability of EU funds, coupled with the relative unavailability of domestic funds, influences the fundraising choices NGOs make. Domestic civil society funding is difficult for advocacy groups to obtain, especially where their work is focused on issues such as human rights. The current culture of giving has not yet familiarized itself with the concepts of advocacy and NGOs. This lack of domestic funding sources creates a natural push for advocacy NGOs to seek external funds.

The chapter offers an outline of domestic funding opportunities in Turkey and juxtaposes this with the system of EU funding for NGOs. The chapter begins with an account of the nature of the funding relationships between donors and CSOs, sketching out the trends in donor aims and the ways in which these aims become operationalized in their funding frameworks. The second section sketches the contours for the overall landscape of civil society funding in Turkey and points out the opportunities and shortcomings this poses for advocacy NGOs. The third section takes a closer look at the domestic actors involved in the operationalization of EU civil society policy. The fourth and final section places the magnifying glass on NGOs, taking account of NGO attitudes and approaches. The argument put forth is that these organizations take very different approaches when faced with the decision of whether to seek external assistance or not. These approaches are contingent on how NGOs view the role of the

EU in Turkey, what their experience of Europeanization has been thus far, and the extent to which the organizations have chosen to either internalize or resist the EU influence upon them. These observations feed into the conclusion that the nature of changes this funding is effectively sponsoring, and the outcomes of EU civil society funding, will remain uncertain.

Donor aims

Donor support for civil society is intricately linked with assumptions about broader processes of development, to which NGOs allegedly contribute with their actions. The underlying argument is one where strong civil society (often referred to as one that is populated by a high number of active CSOs) is seen conducive to a democratic society, and a weak civil society with fewer active CSOs is associated with less democratic states. Additionally, in the EU context in particular, vibrant civil society is expected to assist in the formulation and effective execution of policy. Robert Putnam has echoed these views as he argues that civil society 'inculcates democratic habits' (1995).

Donors see their aims to constitute a neutral, value-free approach, forming a template ready for use in any context (Howell and Pearce, 2001a, pp. 39–40). Yet, aspiring for change in the areas of democratization and policy effectiveness, and seeing NGOs as the preferred civil society partners, clearly forms an agenda in itself. NGOs are favoured due their perceived pro-democratic function of increasing citizen participation in activities that hold the state accountable for its actions. They are also seen to be non-partisan advocates of discussion on neutral issues, moving away from traditional boundaries of political ideology. NGOs can respond well to the bureaucratization and routinization that come with donor funding, and an ability to comply with the bureaucratic minutiae at the heart of donor-funded projects can be interpreted as a neutral, value-free approach (Howell and Lind, 2009, p. 35). This means that a vast majority of the funding programmes end up targeting a small segment of NGOs on the outskirts of local civil society, staffed by youthful, Westernized professional bureaucrats with much common ground with the donors (Carothers, 1999). Such preference for NGOs naturally imposes significant limits to the breadth of CSOs that are considered as potential partners in donor-driven programmes.

While the EU is not the only source of external funding for NGOs in Turkey, it does represent the most prominent donor both in terms of the amount of funding it offers and the attention it has gained from the NGO community. In 2007 the total operating costs of the Open Society Foundation Turkey amounted to $2.3 million. The foundation supported initiatives in EU integration, HIV/AIDS, education reform and promotion of the rights of the Roma. This funding was divided across a number of recipients, including universities, think tanks, hospitals, schools as well as NGOs (Open Society Institute, 2007). German foundations have also been involved in NGO funding. Heinrich Böll Foundation (affiliated with Green politics), Friedrich Naumann Foundation (affiliated with liberal politics), Friedrich Ebert Foundation and Kondrad Adenauer Foundation (both promoting social democracy) all have offices in Istanbul and offer funding towards a range of social activities. Given the strong links with German political parties, these foundations tend to support NGOs with similar political views, however the funding provided is not particularly extensive. It is aimed at facilitating workshops, meetings and general distribution of information, but rarely extends to projects or any long-term financial commitments.[1] Finally, a number of embassies offer small grants to NGOs, but such programmes tend to come and go, as they are often set up by enthusiastic members of staff who receive the support of the current ambassador.[2] Moreover, most of the funders, with the possible exception of the Soros foundation, are very focused on the financial support they offer, and even then offer their funds towards a limited range of activities. It is therefore unlikely that these funders have had significant effect on the role of the EU as the central hub for external funding of NGOs in Turkey.

Domestic funding opportunities for civil society in Turkey

The culture of giving in Turkey combined with the legal framework governing philanthropy makes it more difficult for advocacy NGOs to benefit from domestic funding. The existing contours of domestic funding also help to explain how the overall lack of funds shapes NGO attitudes towards external funding opportunities, such as those provided by the EU. Reliance on short-term, foreign, project-based funding in turn means that their activities are less sustainable in the long term.

In 2005, the *CIVICUS Civil Society Index Report*[3] for Turkey was published which offers a general overview of the state of Turkish civil society (TUSEV, 2005). Soon after, a study titled *Trends in Individual Giving and Foundation Practices* was published that presented the survey and interview findings of the CIVICUS study in more detail (Carkoğlu, 2006). The following box summarizes the key findings from the population survey.

Box 6.1   Summary of key findings from 'Trends in Individual Giving'

- In 2004, individuals donated a total of **$1.910 billion** in Turkey.
- **80%** of the public donate money each year. Of these:
  - o **87%** preferred to give donations directly to individuals, without an institutional intermediary (e.g. NGOs)
  - o **82%** of respondents preferred to support a relative, neighbour or someone from the same region
  - o **70%** of respondents felt it was the responsibility of the state or the most wealthy to look after the needy in society
  - o **70%** were motivated by tax-exemption benefits

Source: Carkoğlu (2006).

While it is somewhat uncertain how accurate these projections are, they nevertheless point to some interesting general observations. For example, given that the data is largely interview based, it is possible that these figures reflect aspirational rather than real donations. First of all, the results speak to the importance of personal connections when making philanthropic donations. The Islamic tradition encourages donations to be made directly to individuals, emphasizing a personal connection with the recipient. The role of institutional intermediaries is minimal, possibly because it cannot add anything to this giving relationship. The results also suggest that the culture of giving stems from a sense of solidarity between the individual donor and the beneficiary, expressing a clear preference to support a relative, neighbour or someone from the same region.

Such culture of giving leaves little room for NGOs to benefit from public philanthropy. This culture, with its origins in the Islamic traditions of giving, constitutes a method of complementing social services provided by the state. In effect, donations serve the purpose of an informal social service, making up for state funds where they are insufficient on their own to provide for the less fortunate. An informal family support network has traditionally supplemented state provision of welfare, and the informal donations made by the public can be regarded as an extension of this system. On the other hand, 70 per cent of the respondents regarded the state as the primary actor in protecting the interests of the least fortunate in society. In between the Islamic tradition of giving with emphasis on a personal connection between the donor and the beneficiary, and the tendency to place responsibility on the state to look after the less fortunate, NGOs are likely to find it difficult to solicit financial contributions from society.

Figure 6.1 elucidates the double bind in which NGOs find themselves. The proportion of funds donated both as direct giving (donations made informally and intermittently to individuals) and

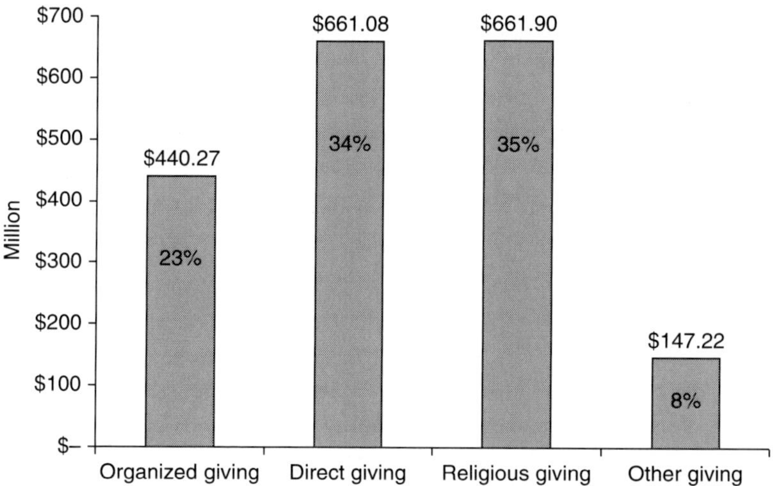

Figure 6.1   Breakdown of total public donations (1910 billion) into four categories
Source: Adapted from Carkoğlu (2006).

religious giving (this includes organized giving to mosques and other religious institutions as fulfilment of religious obligation) is significantly higher than what is given to NGOs in the form of organized giving (formal donations to all non-religious institutions). It is the 'lack of structured funding practices', the CIS report opines, that limits NGO access to funds (TUSEV, 2005, p. 13).

Let's dig a bit deeper into this category of 'organized giving'. Where individuals choose to make donations to CSOs, 19 per cent make their donations to the Turkish Aeronautical Association (*Türk Hava Kurumu* – THK). The THK was established in 1925 by Mustafa Kemal Atatürk and has remained a popular organization to offer donations to. Atatürk attached great importance to aviation, not least because his adopted daughter, Sabiha Gökcen, was the world's first female fighter pilot. Her story became embedded in the broader secular narrative about progress on women's rights, and was taken as evidence of a progressive, modern society that was developing the republic. The THK has thus become a symbol of Kemalism and secularism. It remains the only aviation association in Turkey and traditionally it has been the only organization allowed to receive the skins of animals sacrificed in religious celebrations as donations, and to make an income from this.[4] Thus, a significant portion of the total donations under the organized giving category is taken by one organization alone. In addition, among those who chose to make formal donations to organizations, the three most preferred categories were 'helping the needy, education and helping the handicapped'. The three least preferred causes were 'consumer rights, human rights and animal protection' (Carkoğlu, 2006). In conclusion, the organizations that are likely to find it most difficult to access domestic funds are NGOs that are non-religious and focused on rights-based work.

The previous discussion makes the case that, in the current climate, CSOs – and advocacy NGOs in particular – have limited possibilities for raising funds domestically. There is some real potential within the domestic giving framework that needs to be noted – a genuine interest in philanthropy, indicated by the proportion of population that are active donors each year, as well as by the total amount donated. Yet Turkey is lacking in a culture of philanthropy that would instinctively support NGOs. The prevalence of both ad hoc giving to individuals and religiously organized giving means that donations to secular NGOs are not intuitive, and the avenues for funding these organizations are not clearly marked. Although one should not take funding to be the life and soul of civil society activity, it nevertheless seems reasonable to argue that the potential of advocacy NGOs is encumbered by the unavailability of domestic funding.

NGO views on domestic funding

Interviews with representatives of advocacy NGOs revealed further obstacles to domestic fundraising. Advocacy NGOs' work is perceived as troublemaking by the broader public. Despite working on potentially less political and sensitive agendas – for example, on environmental protection or consumer rights – this still constitutes an agenda for change. The NGO is advocating for change in government policy in order to improve environmental protection measures, for example. Asking for change conveys an underlining message of unhappiness with the present state of affairs – that the government in some way has got it wrong. While this is the essence of what it means to be an advocacy NGO, others often view this position differently:

> Most support goes to health and education because these are safe areas with no controversy because the NGOs are not criticizing the government. Businesses are worried about supporting NGOs that criticize government policy because they might also be labelled as questionable.[5]

> [O]ne very well-known Turkish financier told me that he really would like to support our work, but he was reluctant as he felt this would label him as an 'enemy of the state'.[6]

For NGOs to question or problematize the role of the state in Turkey is often regarded as opposition to the state – not constructive criticism. The public reluctance to support NGOs can be explained, at least in part, by this concern of being labelled troublemakers. Chapter 4 discussed the state tradition of regarding civil society as an ally of secularism and the tendency to bifurcate civil society along the official (secular) and informal (non-secular) lines. Similar dynamics are at play here, where advocacy work is vulnerable to becoming politicized against the polarized, black and white canvas of Turkish politics. It is difficult for NGOs in Turkey to work alongside the state: you are either with the state or against it.

The difficulties NGOs face in achieving tax exemption status illustrates another tricky hurdle in trying to raise money from domestic sources. In order to qualify for tax exemption, each NGO requires an approval from the level of government to assure it is indeed conducting philanthropic work. The minimum standards require all applicants to work in one of the following four areas: education, arts/culture, health or scientific research (TUSEV, 2004a). To date, a mere 700 out of the approximately 80,000 associations in Turkey (0.9 per cent), and 170 of the 4500 foundations (3.8 per cent) have the status of a public benefit organization and are able to return tax exemption gains to their donors (TUSEV, 2005). This has meant that applications for tax exemption from NGOs that focus 'only' on women's issues and not on the public at large have been declined public benefit status.[7]

What to make, then, of the opportunities and shortcomings present within the domestic landscape of civil society funding? While a significant amount of money is donated each year to charitable purposes in Turkey, the way in which it is distributed generates pockets within civil society that are isolated. The areas most affected by funding limitations relate to new types of charitable activity, such as advocacy. These are new in the sense that they have not historically been part of Turkish civil society, or they alternatively are taken to resemble the trouble-making organizations responsible for the political unrest in the 1970s or 1980s and therefore avoided. This need not mean that financial support is the central essence of civil society activity, however, for it is entirely conceivable for NGOs to function effectively with minimal funding, as many do. However, for those advocacy NGOs that deem improved financial support beneficial to their activities, the domestic opportunities for increased funding are very limited. It makes sense, therefore, for such NGOs to concentrate their efforts on funding opportunities available elsewhere.

The EU funding process

This section describes the available funding mechanisms and outlines the role of certain domestic actors that play a key role in channelling funds from the EU to civil society. There are three financial instruments through which Turkish NGOs are able to access EU funding. The main instrument is the budget allocation for pre-accession assistance, an annual allocation of financial support to Turkey directly.[8] This money is channelled to the Turkish government to facilitate the harmonization process in areas such as adopting the EU *acquis* and meeting other requirements for political and economic reform. In 2008 this allocation amounted to approximately €540 million, rising to €654 million in 2010 (see Figure 6.2). In fact, since the start of the pre-accession process in 2004 the annual funding has increased by a factor of 2.5. Within the harmonizing process, funding for civil society falls under the criterion of political reform, where the Turkish government and the EU Delegation in Turkey come together annually to decide on priority areas of funding. All the EU funds available through this instrument are distributed through the CFCU. Another important channel is the Civil Society Development Centre (CSDC), an independent organization that acts as a go-between for the CFCU and NGOs. The roles of both the CFCU and CSDC will be discussed at length later.

The other two financial instruments are linked to the central budget of the EU. These are community programmes and thematic programmes, and Turkish NGOs are eligible to apply for a number of funds within these programmes. The application process for these latter two is located at Brussels, and the funds through these instruments are allocated largely to cooperative projects requiring European partner organizations. While the research discussed here

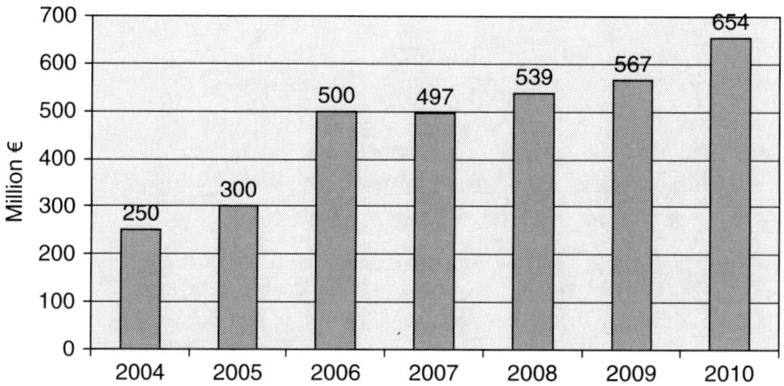

Figure 6.2   Increase in the overall pre-accession funding to Turkey
Source: European Commission (2010a).

focuses on the funding made available within the confines of the pre-accession process (the first financial instrument), it is important to note that other avenues through which NGOs can access EU funding also exist. In particular, this illustrates the complex web of funding channels that NGOs are required to negotiate in the EU context. The process of applying for EU funding is becoming increasingly complicated and many NGOs are finding that access to this complex web of funding channels is beyond their capacity.[9]

The EU Delegation in Ankara emphasizes the need for civil society funding as a way of expanding the impact of the political reforms that are taking place, by extending the political debate to the level of citizens. NGOs are seen as key intermediaries in this process. However, almost no consultation takes place with NGOs on what the priorities ought to be. The ideas for funding are generated internally within the EU Delegation and these are then floated with particular well-known NGOs or in larger roundtable meetings.[10]

It is the EU representatives and the Turkish government who ultimately decide on priorities. The initiative for civil society involvement in decision-making comes from the EU Delegation, not from the organizations themselves. Nor is the process particularly participatory, as NGOs have no role at the early stages of this process when priorities are negotiated. Instead, the consultation meetings become the means of furthering an agenda that has already been decided upon elsewhere. The decision as to how NGOs are supported to take part in the political debate, and through what kinds of projects, is made through a top-down process with minimal consultation.

The medley of three figures (Figures 6.2, 6.3 and 6.4) offer a brief numeric journey through the story of EU funding in Turkey, and give an insight to the way in which financial support is distributed. As Figure 6.2 shows, the amount of financial support has been steadily climbing up throughout the past six years. The first half of Figure 6.3 demonstrates how the total assistance for 2007 was divided between the three main recipients: the EU secretary general (Turkish governmental department responsible for the EU harmonization process), government ministries and civil society. The second half of Figure 6.3 provides a further breakdown of how financing was distributed within civil society.

The relatively sizeable amount of funding received by trade unions and chambers of commerce requires clarification. First of all, this is a clear indication that the EU does not see civil society

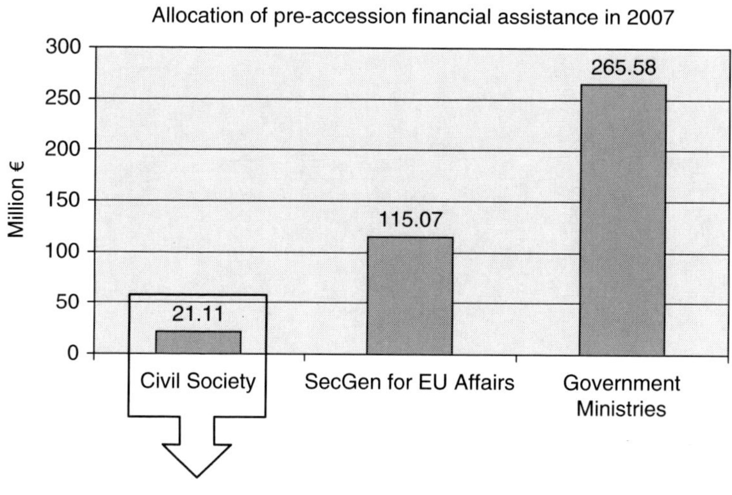

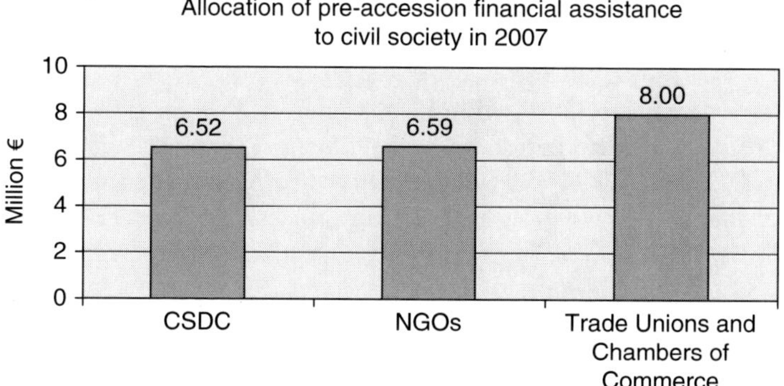

Figure 6.3   Total allocation of pre-accession financial assistance in 2007 (top), and the allocation within this to civil society (bottom)
Source: European Commission (2010b).

only in terms of NGOs. Instead, EU pursues multiple strategies, which in this case involves organizations that are closely linked with economic development. The financial support from the EU was channelled into two large projects, both of which fall under the broader programme of Civil Society Dialogue. One project aimed to strengthen the dialogue and cooperation between the Union of Chambers and Commodity Exchanges of Turkey (*Türkiye Odalar ve*

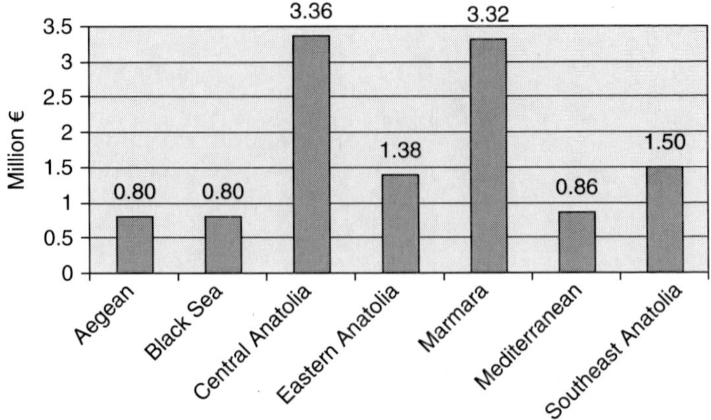

Figure 6.4   Distribution of EU funds by region (Central Anatolia includes Ankara, while Marmara includes Istanbul)
Source: These figures represent the author's own analysis, based on reports provided by the EU Delegation for Turkey.

Bursalar Birliği – TOBB), an umbrella organization with 364 members in Turkey, and the European Association of Chambers of Commerce and Industry (EUROCHAMBRES), thus promoting the integration of Turkish and European business communities (European Commission, 2006a). The objective of the second project was to strengthen contacts and mutual exchange of experience between the trade unions of Turkey and of EU member states. Four national trade union confederations from Turkey were involved (TÜRK-IŞ, HAK-İŞ, DİSK and KESK) as well as confederations from seven European countries (France, Germany, Austria, Italy, Slovakia, Sweden and Greece) (European Commission, 2006c).

Figure 6.4 shows how funding has been distributed across the different regions of Turkey. Although funding reaches all regions there are significant differences in the amount of funding each region receives: Central Anatolia (this region includes funding for Ankara) and Marmara (includes Istanbul) are far ahead of others. A significant proportion of NGOs is located in Ankara and Istanbul, as being near the centres of power makes it easier to gain access to funding.

However, when in Figure 6.5 we reflect on these figures in terms of total populations within each region, the three peaks that emerge in

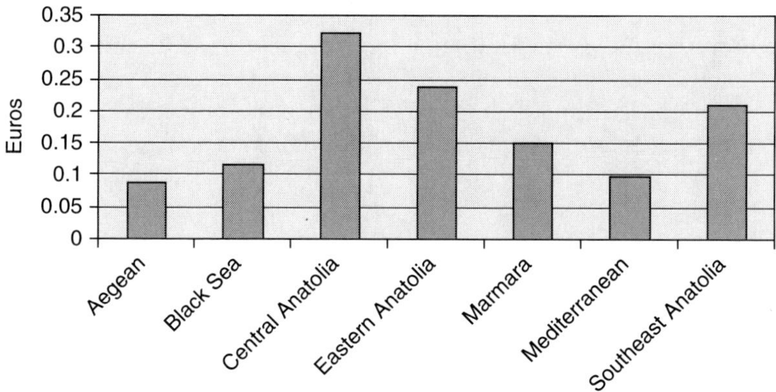

Figure 6.5   Distribution of EU funds per person within each region
Source: Based on population statistics from 2007 (Turkish Statistical Institute, 2010).

Figure 6.4 flatten out somewhat. Although Central Anatolia remains the main recipient of funding, the amount of funding distributed to the Marmara region is more in line with the other regions. In addition, Eastern Anatolia emerges as a region that receives more funding per head than the numbers in Figure 6.4 indicate, joining Southeast Anatolia as a key recipient. Therefore, when we consider EU funding in terms of regional populations, the logic behind the funding strategy becomes clearer. Central Anatolia and Marmara regions receive significant amounts of funding, because these regions are the two most densely populated regions. The two regions in eastern Turkey – Eastern Anatolia and Southeast Anatolia – have relatively low population densities, but in the end receive more funding per head than Marmara region. Furthermore, these eastern regions are among the poorest in Turkey, having suffered from limited investments in infrastructure due to the unstable political situation in the region. These findings suggest that the logic behind EU funding takes into consideration the number of people and the relative need of the population living within a given region.

Domestic intermediaries in the EU funding process

Since the preparations for accession negotiations have begun, the EU has shifted responsibility for many of the procedural operations to Turkish actors. Civil society funding is one such area where the

CFCU and the CSDC have played an important role. These roles offer a useful insight to the changing nature of civil society funding since the start of the negotiations.

The CFCU is the key intermediary, and the most important governmental actor in civil society funding. It is the governmental body with financial oversight over all EU-funded programmes. As has been the case with all recent candidate countries, the CFCU was established as part of the accession negotiations in order to develop an umbrella structure aimed at transferring the contracting authority of the European Commission to the Turkish government. As such, it is part and parcel of the policy Europeanization processes that the accession negotiations have sparked. Since 2003 the CFCU has gradually come to shoulder the responsibility for budgeting, tendering, contracting and all other financial aspects of EU-funded programmes in Turkey, including grants to NGOs. Most of its employees have a background in the civil service, having worked in government ministries or as lawyers and accountants. Many regard this as a simple technical switch, a response to calls to manage the overall funding processes more effectively and to shifting more responsibility onto Turkish institutions – as per the requirements of the pre-accession process. The CFCU is an integral part of the bureaucratic–technical framework of the EU pre-accession process.

The introduction of the CFCU to the funding process denotes a real shift in the EU–civil society relationship. Since the start of the accession process, the EU Delegation in Turkey has developed relationships with a broad variety of stakeholders. Many activities that were previously a direct responsibility of the EU offices in Turkey have been delegated to others. By creating additional levels of administration between the EU offices and the recipient NGOs, the changes have led to a layering effect in civil society funding processes. The shift in the relationship is captured by the following comment:

> Before 2003, when the debate was about reforms required for Turkey to reach the pre-accession stage, we were working closely with civil society actors to steer the agenda and the debate. Once the pre-accession negotiations started, the priority for us shifted from civil society to public institutions that are required to do the actual harmonization work. I don't think the role of NGOs has

changed, but the spectrum has changed, and now they are one among many important actors.[11]

From an NGO perspective, the change that has taken place is more than a technical amendment to operations. The introduction of the CFCU, a third party, to the EU–civil society relationship significantly alters the dynamics. A representative of the CFCU summarized this change in an interview; he said, 'we need to be more rigorous and more detailed in our work because we are looking after someone else's money'.[12] The CFCU is responsible for a broad array of financing, where NGO funding constitutes only a small portion. Furthermore, the CFCU remains primarily accountable to the EU and Turkish ministries to ensure that the money they are channelling is being spent in legitimate ways. Many of the NGO respondents were highly critical of the role of the CFCU in the funding process:

> They are a stupid organization. They are stupid, stupid, stupid. All I do is write reports, fill in forms, work on the accounts. We have now waited six months since we finished our project for the final 20 per cent [€20,000] of the funds to come through.[13]

There are implications for NGOs that arise from this new division of labour and that constitute more than a simple bureaucratic initiative. The way in which the EU Delegation and the CFCU perceive their roles within the funding process is very different, and do not amount to a simple shift of responsibilities from one entity to another. The CFCU is ultimately a government body and it has therefore governmental interests at heart. After all, only a small segment of the funds that flow through the CFCU concerns non-state actors, making NGOs a sideshow for the CFCU. Despite operating in a capacity that is independent of the state, CFCU staff members remain state employees, whose future careers are in part determined by their political affiliations. The state, not the non-state, lies in their direct gaze.

From the point of view of the NGOs, the funding relationship is no longer seen as a partnership with mutual aims. While this shift has been deemed a neutral, administrative operation by the CFCU and the EU Delegation, in fact this can have implications on the ability of NGOs to make use of their comparative advantage: to think outside the box and produce innovative, locally relevant projects. The process constrains them to conduct their work within the strict project criteria governed by forms and reports. While these are not new problems for NGOs in Turkey, the new structures have augmented the magnitude and extent of the difficulties.

The CSDC is a central player in civil society funding. An independent NGO itself, it has established itself as the domestic hub to distribute EU funding in Turkey, as Figure 6.3 indicates. In 2007–8, the CSDC has reportedly issued €3.1 million in grants. Although the project themes still originate from within the EU, the CSDC has considerable discretion over who is being funded. The idea for the CSDC originates from a project funded by the EU Delegation. In 2003, a team of Turkish civil society experts were funded by the EU Commission under a two-year Civil Society Development Programme with the aim of providing NGO training across Turkey. It was following the success of the programme when the team was encouraged by the EU Delegation to form an association and apply for grants. In essence, the CSDC operates as the middleman between the CFCU and the NGOs, a kind of a 'semi-donor'.[14]

The CSDC aims to build the capacity of NGOs at the local level by identifying grantees and offering them support throughout the project cycle. The CSDC staff is Turkish civil society's activists and experts, with locally relevant experience that aims to make the organization more accessible to local NGOs. It is also an attempt to address the inequities of the application process for EU funding, which tends to favour the elite NGOs. The CSDC seems to respond to some of the criticisms that donor-funded programmes have faced, where they are seen as out of touch and imposing an external set of values onto local civil society (Ottaway and Carothers, 2000). In comparison to these observations, the CSDC is a constructive development.

Furthermore, given the origins of the CSDC, it is difficult to consider this entity to be truly an internal mechanism within civil society. The impetus to create the CSDC came from the encouragement within the EU family. The CSDC is not simply part of civil society, just another NGO, but an additional layer in the relationship between the EU and other NGOs. The CSDC offers support and capacity-building services to the NGOs it works with, but it does this in the context of EU-funded projects where the support is aimed at guiding the NGO successfully through the project cycle. In practice, therefore, the actions of the CSDC improve the efficiency of NGOs as vehicles for distributing EU funds and delivering projects. Does the CSDC, therefore, truly help civil society to internalize the new processes EU funding requires, or does it merely perpetuate the superficial nature of external funding?

Earlier in this chapter, as well as frequently throughout the book, the motivations for donor funding towards NGOs have been linked to ideas about democratization and Europeanization. In this regard civil society funding strategies tend to pay special attention to the strengthening of civil society through support for advocacy NGOs. In operationalizing such aims, there seems to be more focus on the management of the funding process and creating channels through which financial assistance is distributed and NGOs made accountable. In Turkey's case this has been realized through intermediary organizations such as the CFCU and CSDC. These developments are illustrative of how Europeanization unfolds in practice but also point to a particular set of circumstances where the processes of change are potentially at odds with the agenda for democratization. Funding for NGOs, despite best intentions by everyone concerned, is unlikely to lead to a more democratic society in any direct, measurable way. Governmental control of the finances for non-governmental action may jeopardize the independence of NGOs. Similarly, the additional layers of management between the EU Delegation and NGOs are likely to increase the distance between the two sides, and compromise the active participation of the latter.

NGO views on the funding process

> Before, you could have projects if you paid from your own money. It was hard, really difficult. In the last ten years the funds have been really good in helping NGOs to really do something.[15]

> We constantly face the question 'who is funding you, who is behind you'. It is important that we can reply that our funds come from members and other supporters inside Turkey.[16]

For NGOs, the attraction of external sources of funding is clear. But what kind of choices will advocacy NGOs make in practice and how do they rationalize their decisions? The argument put forward here suggests that there are two underlying determinants for NGOs to either participate or not in EU-funded programmes: the internal organizational capacity of an NGO and the way an NGO elects to convey its legitimacy as an actor.

Participation in EU funding

Focusing on the internal organizations capacity of NGOs first, this is understood in terms of an ability to carry out activities effectively. From the donor perspective, this idea is strongly linked with the debate on capacity-building. As discussed in Chapter 3 in particular, this can be understood as strengthening the NGO's role in providing services or supporting democratic processes by developing the organizational dimension of an NGO (Lewis, 2001b). From the perspective of Turkish NGOs, the funding they have received from the EU did not change what they did, but it enabled them to do it quicker or do more of it. The NGOs participating in EU-funded projects regarded the assistance as a short cut to achieving aims that previously required a great deal of individual effort. Several examples of the kinds of activities such funding had enabled emerged during the interviews. The additional funds have translated to the creation and dissemination of informational pamphlets about the issues they work on, financial and logistical support for organizing workshops or conferences, support for research projects and publication of research on topical issues such as honour killings.[17] The funding has also improved the organizational capacity of the NGOs, in the more traditional sense of capacity-building.

> Through EU projects we learnt about project management; we had a 'learn by doing' approach to our work which helped us to learn a lot from the EU projects.[18]

Through actions such as hiring staff from a volunteer base, thus avoiding a brain drain at the end of a project, and through the development of managerial and administrative skills during EU-funded projects, internal organizational dimension of NGOs has been a clear beneficiary benefited from EU funding.[19,20] As a consequence, NGOs have become more professional in their activities. Arguably, the support received has made NGOs more viable as organizations. Also, the NGOs partaking in EU-funded projects described the existence of a positive feedback loop where participation in EU-funded projects improves NGO capacity to succeed with future funding applications. On the one hand, this may be the result of increased organizational capacity. On the other hand, the NGOs described themselves as being part of an inner circle that was more likely to succeed with funding applications:

> We find it easy to get funding. Because we have past experience [with EU-funded projects], it helps. The government knows us, the EU knows us – we have some really good contacts. We just do what is needed and we get the money.[21]

In other words, EU support leads to developments outside the immediate terrain of project funding, offering benefits such as increased publicity that in turn helps NGOs to garner additional support.[22] It is a virtuous cycle, where the first two forms of bolstered capacity – effectiveness and organizational strengthening – feed into this third effect. NGOs benefit both internally and externally in terms of publicity and public perceptions that make it more likely to attract more funding from other external sources. Thus the benefits to internal effectiveness motivate NGOs to apply for EU funding in the first instance. The actual experience of participating in funded projects can lead to further improvements, where the positive outcomes of funding both encourage and facilitate further applications for funding. For a group of NGOs, at least, the capacity gains have led to a choice to pursue EU project funding.

The second determinate of NGO participation in EU funding relates to perceptions of legitimacy. Legitimacy refers to the credibility of an organization, based on perceived moral justifications for its social and political actions (Lewis, 2001b, p. 201). In this regard, the EU pre-accession process has been helpful in expanding the spectrum of social and political issues that are deemed legitimate for NGOs to engage in and criticize the actions of the state.[23,24] For example, one respondent commented that 'the EU has had an impact on creating more space for women and gender issues. "Gender" is now part of the EU application process and something we have to address in our applications.'[25]

As discussed in Chapter 4, in this way the EU can offer an external anchor upon which NGOs hinge their efforts (Tocci, 2005). The EU sustains a strong rhetoric in support of human rights and democratization (as discussed in Chapter 3) and the EU interest in these areas has widened the scope of issues that are legitimate for NGOs to work on. Such issues have gained legitimacy as areas of genuine concern, and several NGOs working on issues of environmental rights, child rights and women's rights have begun to make their concerns heard at the national stage. Not only has EU involvement pushed such issues higher up the agenda, but by making the issue of rights an important one, the credibility of organizations working on these issues has also magnified. Both the issue of rights and the NGOs working on rights-based issues have gained credibility through EU involvement.

What is more, the publicity and air of professionalism generated by EU funding also leads to legitimacy gains. It builds an image of a successful organization, a professional organization dealing with genuine issues of concern. Receipt of EU funds becomes shorthand for a successful NGO, and by making NGOs household names, funding from the EU can increase legitimacy of the advocacy work in the eyes of the public. EU funding therefore creates a virtuous cycle – at least for some. EU support leads to gains of both legitimacy and capacity among the recipients, and is advantageous in future applications for funding. However, for other NGOs these two very same issues of legitimacy and capacity can become a criterion for exclusion from EU funding.

Non-participation in EU funding

Continuing on the issue of legitimacy, here the question is how an NGO perceives its source of legitimacy to be undermined by an affiliation with the EU. Several advocacy NGOs consciously avoid donor funding because of this, and even use their opposition to EU funding as a means to garner support for their cause. The decision not to apply for EU funding is part of the organizational mission and sends a message that resonates well with their constituency and the membership of the NGO. If the NGO were to receive money from abroad, this would undermine the justifications for its social and political actions.[26] It would face the possibility that its message would no longer be taken seriously because the NGO would be deemed to be delivering a message on someone else's behalf. As one respondent phrased it, 'Independence is the precondition of being an NGO. External funds give you the label of being the back garden of another organization.'[27] This shadows the old saying 'he who pays the piper calls the tune', alluding to an assumption that an NGO is forced to trade some of its independence in exchange for external assistance.

The decision to avoid external funding is also a reflection on sources of authority. NGOs that position themselves along nationalist or Kemalist political lines source their authority from nationalist/Kemalist political rhetoric, which is in part framed in scepticism over the EU agenda in Turkey. By publicly refusing EU funding NGOs are able to assert their authority as being on the forefront of the nationalist or secular agenda. Contrary to its intentions, EU funding thus provides a potential avenue for anti-EU sentiment to flare up, and offers here an example of how the impact of EU funding reaches beyond the realm of the project. This again highlights some of the uncertainty present in the EU efforts to achieve Europeanization in Turkey.

Secondly, lack of organizational capacity leads NGOs to make the decision not to participate in the EU-funding process. Here the exclusion is not necessarily by choice, but reflects a barrier between EU funding and NGO ability to manage the application and funding processes that surround the funding framework. In the interviews conducted for this research, some NGOs described the gap between their operations and EU funding as unbridgeable. As one respondent commented, 'it's difficult to know enough about the funding process. There are only a few of us and we lack the knowledge.'[28] In a similar manner, other respondents felt that the demands of an EU-funded project were beyond the abilities of the NGO: 'We think the EU projects are too technical, complicated and demanding for us. If we applied, we would have to find someone to carry out the project for us.'[29] These views are confirmed by another respondent who works closely with youth NGOs, supporting their activities:

> The application process [for EU funding] is unbelievable; we no longer think the gains are worth the effort and bureaucracy, especially for inexperienced youth groups. We now advise youth groups not to apply for EU funding.[30]

There are several issues surrounding the application process that lead to NGOs with less capacity to decide not to apply for EU funding. NGOs lack the human resources to cope with the additional work required to find out about opportunities. Second, there are the opportunity costs of conducting the work – the application process in itself is found to be too complex, bureaucratic and not worth the effort. The application process in most cases is in English, which alone is a barrier for many NGOs, regardless of their capacity to conduct the work. Finally, as the previous quotation suggests, EU projects have gained a reputation for being difficult to manage, and for some it is the anticipation of this workload that leads to the decision to avoid EU funding.

There exist various ways that NGOs react to the availability of EU funding. While some NGOs viewed external funding as something to aspire towards, other NGOs had made a conscious decision to completely avoid foreign funding. Reasons for this can be found in NGO perceptions of legitimacy and NGO capacity to apply and manage the projects to which the funding is tied. Despite what seems to be a distinct lack of domestically available funding for advocacy NGOs in Turkey, NGOs do not apply for funding for the sake of it. The way EU funding separates NGOs into participating and non-participating groups should be considered more carefully. These dynamics set the ball rolling in developing a group of elite NGOs that have strong capacity for high impact work, while other NGOs are inadvertently pushed away from these funding opportunities. It is important to think more carefully who in civil society is reached by these funds, what kind of impact this is likely to have, and how these outcomes relate to the announced aims of EU funding. It appears that the way in which project funding is operationalized means that organizations that are bureaucratically obedient and able are preferred.

Funding through projects

This section begins to unpack the way in which projects, the key mechanism for channelling funding, shape NGO behaviour (this discussion continues in more detail in Chapter 7). EU funding to NGOs is distributed solely through projects. The centrality of the project in turn has changed the way NGOs think about their activities, shifting NGO priorities away from their beneficiaries, and shaping the inclusion and exclusion of NGOs in EU-funded projects.

The project approach to funding is highly complex and needs to be carefully deconstructed. Projects are packages of time-constrained activities within a fixed budget, where success and failure are regularly based on quantifiable cost-benefit analysis. While projects can pinpoint money directly to an area where it is needed and ensure that activists with local knowledge are involved, the problem is that most projects are short-lived and often fail to sustain benefits beyond the life of a project. Projects also create dependence by creating a superficial funding environment, spawning groups that only exist because of available funding (Carothers, 1999). Moreover, while projects are being carried out, they often lack flexibility to adapt to a local reality. The monitoring of this work ties NGOs down to writing reports that are unable to convey the local situation. For each project, myriad NGOs apply – how do you pick the right NGO to work with? The tendency is to engage with those NGOs that speak English, particularly the development jargon, and know how to develop project proposals. The fact that all funding is made available through projects in itself acts as a selection criteria for NGOs. The short-termism of project funding also places limits on what kinds of outcomes can be expected.

For those NGOs that partake in projects, or aspire to do so, the experience has certainly shaped them. As one respondent observed, 'projects are increasingly becoming the focus of NGO work. The focus is shifting from voluntary work to having to secure some funding before an idea is worth acting upon.'[31] In a similar fashion another respondent opined, 'the success of NGOs should be dependent on how well they can think "outside of the box". But in reality, their success is measured by how many funds they win.'[32] Both of these comments allude to the same phenomenon. The ideas and actions of NGOs gravitate towards projects, and thus towards types of activities that the EU has decided to fund. These activities are chosen with a view of supporting the Europeanization processes that form the basis of the EU accession negotiations. Although the passion that spurs NGOs to speak for a cause is still there, this is now moderated by a new model as to how NGO work ought to be conducted. The project cycle tends to emphasize the practical needs of running a project and pushes NGOs towards realizing these needs. In the words of another respondent, 'you don't have time to go and implement the project in the field because all your time is taken up by the financial management of the project'.[33]

The way in which NGOs approach funding that is framed around projects has two key outcomes. On the one hand, the projects become a measure of success for NGOs. The application process can be likened to an examination, the passing of which leads to a qualification of sorts. As one interviewee pointed out to me, the language used in this context also suggests this: NGOs 'win' grant 'competitions'.[34] On the other hand, NGO activities are no longer developed organically based on local needs. Instead, the activities become synthetic, designed to meet project criteria. The project competitions are all based on similar ideas, requiring similar activities from the projects; there is no space for NGOs to think outside the box. By becoming the yardstick by which success is measured, projects bring about increased competition among NGOs, potentially fuelling the essentialist nature of civil society activity in Turkey.

What is more, the project approach limits methods of communication between the EU and NGOs to the application process. The NGO communicates its vision of what kind of activities it would like to carry out in a project application, which is then either approved or disapproved by the officials responsible. The nature of the process does not lend itself to a dialogue where, for example, good project ideas that may not be a perfect fit with project criteria, or proposals which are underdeveloped in technical detail but conceptually innovative, are given a chance. A more interactive application process would allow such ideas to be developed, increasing the diversity and breadth of projects as well as helping to make them more locally relevant. In a similar fashion, the communication which takes place between EU representatives and NGOs once a project has been approved displays a similar rigidity. Unfortunately, much of the dialogue is dominated by matters related to financial monitoring, conducted by a third party, the CFCU. In this context, project-based approaches to democratization are rated in terms of financial efficiency and accountability. As long as a project has spent all the money allocated in an accountable fashion, and does so within an agreed time frame, it is hailed as a success. Perhaps it is too soon to expect such well-groomed relationships to have emerged, and with time the dialogue between EU and NGOs may improve. Yet, in the accession context, the EU insulates itself from direct contact by working through third parties such as the CFCU, which perhaps makes such long-term results less likely to materialize.

This is not to say that donors such as the EU should not engage in project-based work. There are good reasons to do so and projects can bring about excellent results. But it is important to be more aware of their limitations and realize what constitutes a realistic expectation in terms of project outcomes. Projects are not a miracle that, when applied to NGOs, can bring about democratization: the broader context matters. Other forms of support are also required, and on the front of democratization, one crucial issue is the mindset of the public towards donating to local advocacy NGOs. Historically, the Turkish public has viewed the state as the only point of call for their grievances and this strong state tradition still prevails to a large extent. Nor is this helped by the generally dismissive attitude by the Turkish state towards the work carried out by advocacy NGOs.

Conclusion

The landscape of domestic funding suggests that advocacy NGOs are drawn to external sources of funding, as support for advocacy NGOs is not yet part of the philanthropic culture in Turkey and therefore domestic sources of philanthropy are channelled in a different direction for the benefit of religious charitable activity and individuals in need. As the accession negotiations began, the EU–NGO relationship in Turkey also changed. Civil society was no longer the key partner for the EU in Turkey, as this role has been taken over by the government. A third party, the CFCU has taken on the task of managing and monitoring the funding process on behalf of the EU Turkey office. These changes have made the process more formal and bureaucratic, focused increasingly on quantifiable end results and on ensuring that funds have been spent in accountable ways. This diverts attention away from the outcome and impact of the funded projects, as they unfold on the ground.

It is important to recognize that among those NGOs that aspire to receive EU funding, at least two groups have emerged. One group has been motivated to internalize the opportunities that have become available. These organizations have gained new skills of project management and learnt how to successfully apply for funding also in the future. The other groups have remained outside of these opportunities, either through a conscious policy of resistance or because project funding does not suit the NGO's circumstances. EU-funding policies are effectively shaping a particular sector of NGOs. Given that certain start-up capacity is required to engage in the funding processes, these groups are more likely to be urban, middle-class, professional NGOs or think tanks that already possess a competitive advantage in carrying out projects. Thus a two-tier system of 'haves and have-nots' (or 'wants' and want-nots' as the case is with those groups that refuse engagement) is gradually established with a core of organizations that are able to deliver projects in a professionalized, bureaucratized manner. Their actions increasingly resemble the actions of a third sector. Thus, the NGOs that participate in EU funding are likely to become involved in the Europeanization processes that have begun in earnest with the start of the pre-accession process.

These observations raise the question of how achievable the objectives behind EU funding are. If the overall objective relates to the development of a vibrant civil society, democratization and Europeanization, as the project documents purport, in what way are these to be achieved by the projects that are funded? One aspect to consider is the possibility that projects are remoulding the way in which NGOs think about their activities. What activities are deemed important and, once engaged, what aspects of these activities are prioritized. Here the answer seems to be that activities selected by the EU to be part of their funding framework are deemed important, and the financial aspect of the project (how money has been spent) is prioritized over qualitative outcomes (how did project beneficiaries feel about their participation and what the long-term implications may be). Since NGO motivations for engaging in funded activities are not necessarily rooted in organizational aims but in the kind of funding that is on offer, it is plausible, although difficult to prove empirically, that NGOs would operate somewhat differently were there no project funding available. Arguably, there is a gap between what projects expect NGOs to do, and how NGOs would naturally operate. How NGOs find ways of reconciling this gap is the focus of the next chapter.

7
Tracing the Impact of EU Policy on the Ground

This final empirical chapter explains how NGOs navigate through the conflicting interests that arise from the incongruence between policy conceptualization and how NGOs operate in practice. The chapter begins with a discussion of the project approach to development, its benefits and shortcomings, and places the actor-oriented perspective (Long, 2001) against the model of rational decision-making that dominates the project-based approach. The actor-oriented perspective has explanatory power because it highlights the complex social processes that inform NGO behaviour in the project environment. Next, to illustrate the agency of Turkish NGOs in the EU project funding context, the chapter draws on the work of Lewis and Mosse (2006) who describe NGOs as 'brokers' and 'translators'. In order to account for the types of roles NGOs have assumed in the Turkish context, two additional roles are conceptualized: 'navigators' and 'antagonists'. Once this framework for thinking about NGO roles from an actor-oriented perspective has been established, the chapter moves on to describe these roles in more detail. Firstly, the role of the CFCU as the representative and executor of EU project policy is explored. The aim here is to illustrate the rational decision-making model that governs the technical management of EU-funded civil society projects. Secondly, the roles NGOs assume as 'translators', 'brokers', 'navigators' and 'antagonists' is surveyed more closely. NGOs, therefore, are not mere passive recipients of project funding. Instead, NGOs react to projects in locally relevant ways, and find ways to negotiate through the funding process in ways that deliver a more favourable (and unanticipated) result for them.

One particular way this inability to anticipate the consequences of social action manifests itself in the context of EU–NGO relations is in the multiplicity of ways NGOs respond to the availability of civil society funding. Thus, while on the one hand social processes are inherently unpredictable, on the other hand it is also possible that actors consciously manipulate the processes for the attainment of their particular ends. In either case, the end result from the point of view of policy planning is the same: the outcomes of the policy processes are uncertain. If we are serious about recognizing the complexity of social interactions and the gap that exists between EU policy and Turkish reality, then we need to investigate the nature of NGOs reactions when they are faced with the choice of participating in EU-funded projects.

The project is identified as a critical juncture where the unanticipated consequences of EU civil society policies in Turkey are located. Projects – particularly the procedures that surround the management of projects – are conceived in ways that prioritize the rational and scientific assumptions about what projects are meant to achieve, and how their success in achieving these goals are best measured. Projects, however, do not take place in a rational vacuum, but are rooted in the local social context. From this local context emerge diverse ways for local actors to relate to projects. It is therefore important to focus on the interaction between local NGOs and the EU in order to understand what kind of unanticipated consequences EU project finance can generate.

Projects and rational problem solving

In development work, projects are rarely regarded as particularly effective tools for altering human behaviour. They have often been criticized for imposing a linear and technical way of thinking, drawing a straight line between a problem and the policy designed to address it (Ferguson, 1990; Fowler, 1997; Mosse, 2004). Yet projects have remained the dominant force for engaging NGOs in donor-funded programmes (Tvedt, 1998). Arguably, the emphasis on projects has receded in recent years, as donors have become increasingly aware of the need to coordinate their funding efforts. In 2005 the Paris Declaration on Aid Effectiveness[1] aimed to improve the harmonization of aid objectives and delivery procedures, all in an effort to improve aid effectiveness (DFID, 2009; Foresti, Booth and O'Neil,

2006). While donor emphasis has shifted from discrete projects towards broader programmes, within these programmes projects still remain the primary mode of channelling funding to local actors, such as NGOs. This is certainly the case with EU funding in Turkey. The intervention offered by the project is a pre-planned set of actions with anticipated outcomes, which does not correspond to the reality of NGO work on the ground. Instead, we should see the project as part of an ongoing process, whose success is dependent on the broader context in which the actors engaged in the project operate.

Donors tend to see projects as an integral part of a rational method for finding a way to implement a given policy agenda. The logical sequence of activities – setting the policy agenda, identifying the problem on the basis of this agenda, designing a policy intervention that is aimed at dealing with the problem, implementing the policy, and evaluating its success – surrounding the project has its advantages as far as fund-disbursing mechanisms go (Long, 2001). It allows donors to embed accountability measures in their funding programmes, which is an important aspect of EU funding given that the financial resources for the project originate from the EU taxpayer. Projects have predefined objectives that NGOs promise to fulfil, time constraints by which NGOs promise to abide, and detailed budget frames that specify how the grant money can be spent along with quantifiable outcomes against which success is measured. It would be unrealistic to expect these conditions not to exist. For the NGOs, these requirements offer a concrete way to demonstrate success and at the same time donor expectations are made transparent. From a donor's perspective, projects simplify the complex process of social change into bite-sized chunks that are more easily managed (Fowler, 1997), making them an attractive option to fund.

However, the logical sequence of activities discussed previously does not always match up with the logic of activities on the ground. A key issue in donor policy is precisely the fact that the policymaking agenda is established prior to problem identification. This order of events means that the policy agenda – such as the agenda for democratization or the agenda behind civil society dialogue, both of which were discussed in Chapter 3 – acts as a filter to the possible ways in which the problem is going to be conceptualized or understood. Agenda-setting thus becomes a critical point in the process because the chosen agenda influences all subsequent decisions regarding policy preferences, even where it differs from the ground-level issues it aims to address (Lukes, 1974). Lack of congruence between the broad agenda and the issues on the ground means, in this case, that there is likely to be a gap between EU policy and NGO reality.

The rational approach to projects favoured by donors is based on certain assumptions about the nature of planned interventions that need to be dissected. The project is assumed to form a discrete set of activities that sets aside a time and space 'bubble' where the intervention is supposed to take place. In other words, it is isolated from 'the continuous flow of social life and ongoing relations that evolve between the various social actors' (Long, 2001, p. 32). Interventions that aim to alter human behaviour need to appreciate that the existing behaviour is a product of a long chain of events, suggesting that successful projects must actively engage with the historical and social context where they are located. Given the logical–rational mindset behind projects, they tend to have an innate focus on formal structures and organizations, making it difficult for these issues to be considered. The informal rules and practices that shape the context in which a project takes place get sidelined (de Zeeuw, 2005, p. 500). NGOs that adopt a narrow project focus can become vehicles pursuing donor agendas that lack relevance to what is needed (Eade, 2007). Having been developed by donors, projects are also more likely to reflect donor interests. We can then surmise that success is likely to be determined on the grounds of how closely projects resemble donor policy models (Mosse, 2005).

The actor-oriented approach has been developed on the basis of such a critique, moving away from emphasis on structural and rational strategies and, instead, considering the relationship between policy and practice as 'a messy free-for-all in which processes are often uncontrollable and results uncertain' (Lewis and Mosse, 2006, p. 9). In the context of development projects, the actor-oriented approach endeavours to develop a conceptual framework that is more attentive to the contextual nuances and offers a useful starting point for considering the uncertainty of outcomes. Key principles of the approach can be summarized as follows:

- Social life is heterogeneous. It comprises a wide diversity of social forms and cultural repertoires, even under seemingly homogeneous circumstances.

- It is necessary to study how such differences are produced, reproduced, consolidated and transformed, and to identify the social processes involved, not merely the structural outcomes.
- In order to examine these interrelations it is useful to work with the concept of 'social interface' which explores how discrepancies of social interest, cultural interpretation, knowledge and power are mediated and perpetuated or transformed at critical points of linkage or confrontation.
- Thus the major challenge is to delineate the contours and contents of diverse social forms, explain their genesis and trace out their implications for strategic action and modes of consciousness. That is, we need to understand how these forms take shape under specific conditions and in relation to past configurations, with a view to examining their viability, self-generating capacities and wider ramifications.

Long (2001, pp. 49–50)

Social interface is a key concept within the actor-oriented approach, looking at the points of linkage where external factors become internalized by local actors. It is useful here because it offers a method of entering the black box of what actually happens when policy gets implemented through a project – projects being one such interface where external and local actors engage with each other (Latour, 1999). A key part of an analysis based on the actor-oriented perspective is to understand the interaction between the various actors; to show how the interest groups, through negotiation, interpret the processes surrounding a planned intervention differently (Long, 2001, p. 72). This style of inquiry asks us to pay attention to the diversity, discrepancies and uncertainty that are present in development interventions.

The approach, however, has been critiqued for being too focused on formal interaction and negotiation between the external and local actors. It places the spotlight on understanding the strategies actors adopt without taking into consideration the impact of the broader context in which actors operate. The focus on points of linkage – on formal interactions and negotiations – places unnecessary limits on how we should understand the way in which local actors operate. While the actor-oriented approach has made an important contribution by communicating a persuasive critique of the structural–rational approach to development, and is therefore an invaluable stepping stone towards a more sociologically oriented understanding of donor-funded projects, there are strategies and methods of acting that are not explained by what takes place in the social interface. As Lewis and Mosse insightfully observe, 'it is the appearance of congruence between problems and interventions, the coherence of policy logic, and the authority of expertise that is really surprising and requires explanation' (2006).

It is in this vein that Lewis and Mosse introduce the ideas of 'brokerage' and 'translation' as concepts that complement the work initiated by the actor-oriented methods. This is aimed to push the analysis further, to consider both the agency of the actors involved as well as the influence of existing power structures on these actors. It is therefore not merely a case of looking at how external factors are internalized, but also how this works the other way around – how internal factors may become externalized.

Brokers, translators, navigators and antagonists

Conceptualizing NGO roles through these four lenses enables one to demonstrate the agency NGOs have as actors within the project framework. It is not a top-down relationship, where NGOs participate in projects as mere vehicles implementing policies conceived by donors. The NGOs respond in various ways to the opportunities and challenges a project brings to them. Secondly, this approach considers NGOs as products of the socio-cultural context where they operate, creations of the broader structures within which they exist. Brokers, translators, navigators and antagonists function in the intermediary terrain between the funders and the local fund beneficiaries, internalizing the system of funding and making it meaningful in the local context.

The concept of translation emphasizes the dynamic nature of the social world, where the meaning of ideas is constantly reshaped, transformed and translated (Latour, 2005). The notion of translation therefore problematizes policy, seeing it as a continuous process of transformation and translation (Lendvai and Stubbs, 2009). The acceptance of new (policy) ideas is not solely dependent on the initial influence of agenda-setting. Instead, the system is dependent on the willingness of others to take up the idea and transfer it further (Latour, 1986). Translators, then, reinterpret the original idea and its meaning on the basis of their own interests and understandings. Viewing civil society actors as translators offers a useful lens through which to reflect more deeply on the donor–NGO relationship. The purpose of adopting this point of view is to move beyond the functions NGOs have inside existing funding frameworks and to understand how projects in reality create new and translated forms of behaviour. In other words, translation explores one particular way in which Europeanization unfolds on the ground and resonates strongly with the sociological institutionalist approach.

It is indeed important to consider these issues in the context of the broader processes of policymaking of which EU funding to civil society is a part. The notion of translation offers a persuasive critique of policy transfer literature, and in particular of the Europeanization literature that sees European integration as a rational and linear process (Lendvai and Stubbs, 2009). In a classic model of European integration, 'goodness of fit' is regarded as the starting point for a process of domestic structural change that leads to an improved fit, thus achieving greater integration (Risse, Cowles and Caporaso, 2001). Furthermore, this point of view connects with the rational project approach that has been adopted in the funding programmes that support these processes of change. In their raw form, the interests championed by Turkish NGOs may be contradictory to the aims of EU civil society funding. Conceptualizing the acts of NGOs as translation highlights the process of finding a way of reconciling their various contradictory interests with the aims of donor-funded projects. These actions bridge the potential disconnect between policy documents that prescribe solutions and the reality on the ground. Lewis and Mosse offer three examples of the types of tools NGOs make use of in translating interests: research, workshops and reports (2006, p. 164). In addition, examples in this chapter illustrate how projects and project implementation offer more space for translation to take place.

Viewing NGOs as brokers offers an insight into how actors find a way to make the system work for them. Brokerage can be understood to mean 'social actors situated at the interface of two socio-cultural universes, and endowed with the capacity to establish links among themselves, be they symbolic, economic, material or political' (Sardan, 1999, p. 37). These 'intermediaries' (Lendvai and Stubbs, 2009) connect and facilitate the relationships between the actors that come together in the funded project interface. They are 'entrepreneurial agents' (Lewis and Mosse, 2006, p. 13) who carve out a role for themselves from within the processes that surround project funding. Viewing these actors as brokers locates their role in the broader cultural and political context. Broker does not refer to a new role generated purely out of the opportunities made available by project funding. Instead, they make use of the already existing entrepreneurial instincts that have been developed as a survival mechanism in a context where weak state and weak institutions leave actors unable to depend on formal processes. In the case of Turkey, the logic of brokerage operates through a reinterpretation of existing practices in ways that suit the new possibilities brought about by the presence of the EU. The concepts of brokers and translators help us to delve deeper into the ways in which Turkish NGOs operate in the mid-terrain between local realities and the policy environment created by EU funding.

Explaining NGO behaviour in the Turkish context requires two additional categories to fully account for NGO actions – navigators and antagonists. Brokering and translation focus on actions of NGOs as intermediaries that are positioned in between two sets of actors and find ways to reconcile the divergent views between them. The roles of navigators and antagonists approach the issue from a different angle, focusing on the strategies that help NGOs reconcile their own work with donor demands. Navigators identify innovative ways to narrow the gap between the current portfolio of skills they can offer and what is required by successful applications for EU projects. Antagonists' roles are marked by their refusal to engage. The EU–NGO relationship is therefore not only marked by possibilities for reinterpretation and choice – as outlined by the first three roles – but also by normative disagreements that make working together difficult. Yet these kinds of responses are not wholly negative for NGOs. The decision not to engage is not a simple case of disagreement but remains a positive or generative act for the NGO, as NGOs that employ such strategies find them beneficial.

EU funding for projects in Turkey

The development project can be likened to a complex machine. When the machine works efficiently, the internal complexity of the machine is not of concern (Latour, 1999). Similarly, in rating the success of a development project the focus has remained more on the quantifiable, often meaning financial, inputs and outputs of projects. The bureaucratic accountability for how money has been spent has become the priority focus for assessment. Arguably, the actual mechanics of the processes that lead to success remain 'opaque and obscure' (Lewis and Mosse, 2006, p. 15).

Recent efforts by the donor community to reform the global structures for providing aid have reinforced the mechanisms for focusing on predefined outcomes and bureaucratic accountability mechanisms. The 'Paris Declaration on Aid Effectiveness' is a case in point. Adopted in March 2005 and reiterated by the 'Accra Agenda for Action' in 2008, the declaration set forth five broad principles. The first three – ownership, alignment and harmonization – called for recipient countries to be able to decide on the content of the aid agenda, alignment of national development strategies with aid programmes, and coordination of donor efforts that avoids duplication in the demands donors make on local governments. The last two – managing for results and mutual accountability – ask for aid to be managed in ways that focus on desired results, as well as in ways that ensure donors and recipient countries are mutually accountable to each other for the results of aid (DFID, 2009; Foresti, Booth and O'Neil, 2006; OECD, 2008). The impact of the latter two principles in particular is felt directly at the level of NGOs, expressed through the emphasis within development projects on results-orientation and accountability through bureaucratic measures. Developments in a similar direction are also visible in the Turkish context.

The EU pre-accession process introduced a new layer of management in the NGO enterprise. The bureaucrats working in the CFCU are the engineers that look after Latour's metaphorical machine, and embrace a role that focuses on project inputs and outputs. The CFCU acts as the middleman between EU institutions and Turkish NGOs. It was set up as part of the EU pre-accession process to oversee all of EU financial support towards Turkey's accession process and remains the organization that is at the heart of project funding, tasked with tendering, evaluating, contracting, accounting, payments and reporting. In other words, the CFCU is responsible for overseeing the completion of the entire project cycle (CFCU, 2009). Given its role as a middleman, it is important to pay attention to the apparent disconnect that exists between how the CFCU and NGOs operate.

One of the key concerns for the CFCU is accountability. It is essentially a Turkish organization that has been given responsibility to look after EU money, and for this reason the CFCU takes its role as an accountant very seriously. Interviews with CFCU staff also highlighted the rigorous guidelines that govern what the CFCU can and cannot do. Because they are contracted by the EU Delegation in Turkey to monitor a wide range of EU-funded initiatives, financial accountability is the key concern for CFCU.[2]

The guidelines require, for example, that all projects tendered with a value of €10,000 or more are accompanied by a logical framework and a concept note document. The budgets that come with project proposals have specific rules about how the grant money should be allocated under the different areas of the project, such as human resource costs and administrative costs. During ongoing projects, the CFCU holds frequent meetings with the NGOs involved to ensure that accounts are kept in good order and they agree to release money for the next phase of the project only when the accounts for the previous phase have been checked and approved. The CFCU speaks highly of the much improved 'commitment ratios' for NGOs, which refer to the percentage of the total funding made available by the EU that is successfully invested in projects. The CFCU puts this improvement down to a change in policy: projects that fail to live up to budget requirements are no longer failed at the outset, but offered assistance by the CFCU in order to balance their budgets according to the rules. The CFCU is also required to report biannually to the European Commission on its activities. It is these accountability processes that take centre stage in the role the CFCU assumes in its relationship with NGOs. Such issues dominate daily project management. As long as the project unfolds as the project proposal anticipated, in accordance with the proposed logical framework and the financial spending plan, it is expected to make a positive contribution and regarded as a success. The concerns for accountability point upwards, towards the EU, leaving NGOs to battle with requirements that have little practical resonance with how they operate.

NGOs make up only a small part of the CFCU's mandate. In fact, a majority of the CFCU work involves overseeing the financial contracts of EU funding to ministries and other public bodies, and the work done with NGOs follows similar guidelines for accounting and reporting. The procedures do not allow flexibility for the fact that many NGOs are often run on a volunteer basis, with staff that work part-time and lack the capacity to deal effectively with the accounting aspect of project management. Therefore the NGOs find it very demanding to comply with the requirements and feel that the way in which the CFCU operates reflects an unawareness of the way in which NGOs carry out their work, and as a result the CFCU engagement hinders rather than helps the NGOs.

There were of course similar measures in place before the CFCU became operational, but the official start of the accession process and the creation of the CFCU have further formalized and bureaucratized the operationalization of NGO funding. Returning to the idea of projects as an interface, a linkage between two lifeworlds (Long, 2001), the introduction of the CFCU into the relationship has made the linkage between the logic of EU funding and NGO work increasingly tenuous. The attitudes and interests that come face-to-face in the project interface are more incongruent. The widening gap in turn augments the space for interpretation through various forms of brokerage and translation. The next section peers inside the 'black box of the project' in order to better understand the choices that NGOs make and the strategies they adapt when faced with the idea of EU project funding.

NGOs at the project interface

The aforementioned bureaucratic demands related to NGO project management solicit a variety of reactions from Turkish civil society actors. The concern with measurable outcomes that dominate the EU-funding agenda is something NGOs view, and therefore react to, in a variety of ways. They either embrace this agenda and manipulate it to their own advantage, or deem it as a method of control that needs to be resisted, even actively undermined. As they do so, these organizations embrace, appropriate or reject the project mentality that EU funding introduces. These reactions arise from the fact that there is a disconnect, a gap, in the social interface that projects constitute. Out of this disconnect arise opportunities for local actors to generate new ways of conducting their work, new ways of bridging the discrepancies that exist between the EU policy logic and what actually happens. It allows one to widen the scope of study beyond the linear relationship between inputs and outputs of a project and to appreciate the much broader range of outcomes that need to be considered and how these come about. The disconnect also leads to questions over the appropriateness of project-based support as a means of bringing about change. In Turkey's case, projects are more concerned with the bureaucratic needs of the accession process than with the needs of civil society. Next, these issues are addressed by looking at the roles NGOs take as translators, brokers, navigators and antagonists.

NGOs as translators

The characteristics of a translator are crystallized in the operations of the CSDC. Its role has rather literally been to translate the EU-driven ideas about civil society funding to suit Turkish reality. As Chapter 6 already described in some detail, the centre itself was initially set up as an EU project. The original aim in setting up the CSDC was to locate it half-way between local NGOs and the EU-funding programmes. To this end the centre has run its own project application programme and been responsible for selecting which projects it wishes to fund. Staffed by Turkish civil society activists with long experience of working in the field, the CSDC offers advice and support on project management and, in so doing, opens the door for less capable NGOs to access funding. Through its operations the CSDC works towards a locally relevant vision of the EU-funding agenda. The centre has embraced the way in which the EU operationalizes its civil society funding, while at the same time working to reinterpret the purpose of its activities and role so that it fits in better with local needs. It is a prime example of a local actor as translator, an organization that has taken up the ideas and actions introduced by EU funding and then renegotiated these further in an effort to reshape their meaning in a way that is more contextually relevant.

The outcomes of the first two CSDC Advisory Board meetings, held in September 2005 and April 2006, offer an insight to how such reinterpretation takes place. The meetings were organized with a view to solicit opinions about the course that the CSDC was following. Over 80 NGOs participated in both meetings, and two documents outlining the outcomes have been published on the CSDC website (CSDC, 2005, 2006).[3] In the first meeting, the agenda focused on the theme of 'problems for NGOs in Turkey'. The second meeting focused on the activities the centre engages in (e.g. training and other NGO support activities, such as grants) and how these could be improved. In terms of civil society development, these notes reveal a desire for civil society to find a more united, collective voice. The participants lament the fragmented relationships and communication that exist between NGOs, and the subsequent lack of common objectives and inability to speak with one voice. This is seen as a necessary development in order for civil society to become a more capable and influential voice in society. In brainstorming how the CSDC could contribute to resolving these issues the following suggestions were made by the participants: branching of CSDC, organizing workshops that allow NGOs to come together, organizing meetings around common agendas (such as EU-related issues), helping NGOs to establish a communication strategy, publishing a book on best practices for NGOs as well as a director–leader handbook, and providing training on internal communications and lobbying to help NGOs participate in relevant EU platforms.

The notes from the two meetings describe how local actors are interpreting local needs in ways that can realistically be addressed through the framework offered by EU civil society funding. The meetings were an exercise in matching the concerns of the local civil society actors with possible solutions from within the EU-funding framework. This is evident from the style of approach, where the solutions that are proposed – expansion of CSDC, organizing meetings or training sessions and development of publications – are all practices that are usually introduced by donor policy (there are today four regional branches of the CSDC). The meetings could therefore be described as translation exercises where local interests were reinterpreted to suit the EU-led agenda for civil society development.

How the Advisory Board conceptualized the problems and needs of Turkish civil society offers further evidence of translation. The problems were identified on the basis of a particular idea of what civil society means, an idea which resonates strongly with the European concept of civil society. For example, identifying the lack of a collective voice as a problem, and aspiring for civil society to gain greater influence by developing a united voice closely correlates with the liberal view of civil society promoted by the EU (and discussed in more detail in Chapters 2 and 3). Lack of volunteerism and local participation, as well as competition between NGOs, were among the other problems that also resonate with the Western ideas about civil society. Similarly, the very concept behind the CSDC originates from a similar understanding of civil society. It may be unreasonable to expect the members of the Advisory Board to engage in problematizing the role of the CSDC as a civil society actor. Yet the fact that the CSDC is accepted as an idea by local actors suggests that an act of translation has already occurred.

These discussions and the indication they give of the broader role of the CSDC serve as a good example of how civil society actors in Turkey engage in reconciling EU ideas for civil society development with the Turkish reality. The CSDC thus plays a translating role as a middleman between EU efforts to fund civil society and the NGOs on the ground that undertake the work through projects. It offers examples of how the policy design – training, workshops, publications and, above all, projects – through which donors operationalize their vision for civil society, is translated to better suit a local context. The actions here show that EU policy and reality of Turkish civil society do resonate with each other, and the processes of Europeanizing Turkish civil society is also driven by an internal motivation. Given this role, the practices in which the CSDC engages as an organization characterize the trend towards Europeanization of Turkish civil society.

NGOs as brokers

In their engagement with project funding, Turkish NGOs have displayed an ability to create new roles for themselves and not simply follow the normative guidelines that the EU rules for civil society funding prescribe. These brokering roles are produced by the new situation in which NGOs find themselves as they respond to changing circumstances and hope to bridge the gap that exists between the organization and access to EU funding. Such a point of view allows us to see the entrepreneurial character of NGOs and elaborates on the variety of possible responses through which civil society can shape the outcomes of EU involvement. This section outlines one of the unexpected ways in which NGOs have reacted to the increasing availability of project funding. In so doing, it suggests that the impact of EU funding is more wide-reaching and complex than anticipated, leading to uncertain and uncontrollable results.

In response to the rise of project funding, an industry of consultancies acting as brokers has also emerged. Some regard these simply as a support network that less capable NGOs can rely on, levelling the playing field and providing English language or project preparation assistance wherever lacking inside the NGO.[4] The CFCU, however, has taken action against consultancies that have branded themselves as 'CFCU accredited', taking out advertisements that warn NGOs no such accreditation exists.[5] However, these consultancies are very creative with identifying gaps in the system, for example, by recruiting well-known civil society activists to act as the figureheads on project applications and in this way getting around the scrutiny that would otherwise have prevented them from winning projects.

> We [EU Delegation] don't give funding to new companies that all of a sudden spring up. But [the consultancies] were able to recruit to their companies figures from civil society who had been committed to one particular field for so many years, and all of a sudden you look and see that this person is now in this company.[6]

The involvement of these consultancies has had a significant impact on the outcomes of EU-funded projects. The director of the CSDC had an encounter with a consultancy that is worth recalling here. He received a phone call enquiring about upcoming grant programmes for NGOs. As the caller was working for a consultancy, the director explained that only NGOs were eligible to apply. The caller said he knew this, and their role was to design projects for NGOs – they had so far created 48 projects, four of which had been sent to the CSDC:

> I checked our database and saw that the proposals they submitted before had been accepted. Twice. I looked in the computer and saw the logical frameworks in these proposals were the same; they only changed the cover page! When I went to visit one of these NGOs, I asked, 'So you will soon start a project. What kind of preparations have you made?' He said, 'Oh, I don't actually yet know what kind of project we are going to make. The consultancy made the application; we just said that we will cooperate with them.'[7]

The NGO had simply agreed to pay the consultancy a fee of 10 per cent of the value of the award. The project budget has no such allocation available, yet the NGO thought they could find a way to spend the money in this way. Here we can observe two separate acts of mediation. One is the role played by the consultancy as a broker. It identifies the gap between the EU project culture and the local NGO culture and offers its services as a way to bridge this gap. The second is by the NGO that recognizes its own lack of capacity to apply for EU funding yet is able to identify a path that will gain it access to EU funds.

NGOs as navigators

The term 'navigator' refers to the ability of NGOs to identify opportunities to access donor funds, utilizing the funding process to their own ends and finding ways to make the funding framework work for them. Navigator NGOs display the same entrepreneurial spirit as broker NGOs, but aim it at different outcomes. While brokers act as go-betweens that bridge the donor reality with local reality, navigators use entrepreneurial skills to take advantage of the opportunities donor funding generates, and do so for their own ends. In this sense their actions are opportunistic – the NGOs find ways to navigate through the differences that exist between their current state of affairs and accessing funds. NGOs begin the process from the amount of funding available, and create a set of activities that fit the amount of funding available. Only afterwards do they identify the mission and the main goal that fits with these activities, turning the project planning process back to front.[8]

The case of an Istanbul-based human rights organization demonstrates how NGOs can make EU funding work for them. They have set up a separate association, used for their official work, such as applying for donor funding. A friend of the director working for the EU Delegation in Ankara suggested that the organization apply for a grant. The application proposed to create a new human rights centre, which was successful. However, the creation of the centre brought no change to the daily operations of the NGO. In order to convince the EU Delegation to grant the funding, they had to describe the purpose of the funds as creating a new centre for human rights. They simply packaged some of the NGOs existing work as the centre's activities. This way the project had a concrete end result that appealed to the funders.[9] The actions exemplify how NGOs find ways to navigate a path towards a situation where it is able to benefit from NGO funding, even where its initial circumstances may not have been favourable for such an outcome, and identify new opportunities for funding. The NGO had found a way to package their work so that it was granted access to EU funding without compromising its own interests. The examples demonstrates the skills NGOs have in reinterpreting their own work in ways that make it relevant to the funding agenda of donors.

A women's NGO in Diyarbakir that was established by the local municipality is another organization that exhibits these entrepreneurial navigation skills. In the 1990s, vast numbers of internally displaced people[10] from the southeast of Turkey gravitated to Diyarbakir, and women previously accustomed to life in villages have faced difficulties in becoming economically productive in an urban environment. The NGO helps immigrant women to become economically active again. In effect, it is an example of how the Diyarbakir municipality has 'branched out' by setting up its own bespoke women's NGO.[11] This NGO acts as a partner organization in an EU-funded project aiming to integrate internally displaced people. In fact, one aim of the EU project is to bring together municipal and NGO actors in order to establish closer links between local government and civil society (for a more detailed discussion see Chapter 5). It is the only partner NGO involved in the project. The funding supports the construction of a new complex where vocational training as well as support services for the disabled, women and children will be housed. The NGO acknowledges its close relationship with the municipality. This partnership is likely to remain in place for a relatively long time, for the NGO is cognizant of the problems of long-term funding and anticipates that the municipality will also be the source of future funding. This example again illustrates how local actors identify the gaps between their current method of operations and what is required in order to access EU funding. It is an example of how NGOs are able to carve out new roles for themselves, defining new limits for how EU funding can be approached.

Such 'invented' NGOs could in fact form a separate, fifth category in this analysis. However, while inventing an NGO purely to gain access to project funding is admittedly a rather radical and unique solution, at the same time it can be regarded as another example of the ability of local actors to identify innovative ways through which to be offered funding, even when they should not qualify for it. For this reason invented NGOs remain here as an example of the entrepreneurial spirit that NGOs exhibit when they are looking for ways to access EU funding, justifying its categorization as a subset of navigators. Nevertheless the implications of such invented NGOs warrant a brief discussion here. It raises questions about what exactly can be achieved with the help of external funding, and what we can extrapolate from the numerical strength of the NGO sector in terms of development of civil society as an active force in Turkish society and politics. This example certainly questions the link often made between NGO funding and democratization, something that was explored in Chapter 3 in relation to EU policy. Furthermore, we need to ask who the beneficiaries of such an NGO are and what position does such organization hold in the local community. The assumptions underlining EU policy explored in Chapter 3 expect NGOs to gain their legitimacy from the communities they represent, and this is also the logic behind the perceived democratizing effect of NGOs. Yet, at the same time, the invented NGO, given its close relationship with the municipality, may possess many of the administrative and bureaucratic skills relevant to completing EU projects that may be important to successfully achieve project outcomes.

NGOs as antagonists

When faced with the possibility of applying for EU project funding, some NGOs pursue an entirely different type of strategy. So far, the discussion has focused on ways in which NGOs engage in the processes that the EU has in place, either by embracing and translating, by brokering or by navigating the system so that it makes sense in the local context. However, it is also worth exploring the resistance that NGOs display towards the EU. This is a form of extreme brokering that is distinct from the forms discussed earlier, in that the strategies are premised on disengagement with the EU.

Take for example one republican women's NGO interviewed in Ankara. This NGO takes a stance against EU funding. It does this on the basis that external funding poses a challenge to the independence of civil society. Institutions such as the EU have a particular agenda that they wish to implement in Turkey, and NGOs are being asked to help with the implementation. The funding is therefore viewed as not being neutral; there is deemed to be an agenda behind it that goes beyond merely funding and spills over into attempts to control NGO behaviour.[12]

Politically the NGO can be described as conservatively secular, at least to the extent that it opposes the proposals to allow the wearing of the headscarf in universities and other public spaces, and the NGO participated actively in the demonstration in the spring of 2007 (these demonstrations were discussed in some detail in Chapter 4). This is not to say they are not progressive, for the NGO was also at the forefront of pushing through the groundbreaking reforms regarding Turkish Penal and Civil Codes that were described in Chapter 5. The NGO respects all work done by other NGOs that do receive foreign funding, and they can see the positive results, yet they themselves refuse foreign funding on the grounds that it comes with a hidden agenda. This attitude reinforces a broader set of issues that relate to scepticism and weariness towards the EU accession process. The refusal to accept EU funding contributes to the organizational identity of this NGO. The act of antagonism is therefore a generative act; it produces a positive outcome for the NGO. The resistance to EU funding is viewed as a source of integrity, as a visible sign of keeping true to the values they uphold as an organization.

A Muslim human rights organization takes a similar stance on the issue of foreign funding. There is no strict overarching policy for the whole organization whereby EU funding is refused. The organization consists of over 20 branches that are located all around Turkey, where each branch can take its own approach to the use of external funds. The branch from Diyarbakir has adopted a policy of not applying or accepting any foreign funding because of the way this was likely to undermine their work:

> Independence, this is a precondition of being an NGO. Domestic funds from government or from other groups within the country give you the label of being the back garden of another organization. This issue is taken very seriously in Turkey.[13]

Accepting funds from outside would taint the reputation of the NGO and politicize it in an undesirable way. Given its geopolitical location in the Kurdish heartland, the organization felt it extremely important to display political neutrality in their work and to show that they were concerned with the issue of human rights only. Acceptance of EU funding would have allowed others to politicize their work and to argue that their work was not about defence of human rights but also about, for example, the politics of Kurdish and/or Muslim issues in Turkey. Hence, both organizations – the women's NGO from the previous example and the Muslim human rights NGO – reject funding because of political reasons, although the motivations to do so were very different. In the latter case the underlying strategic reason for refusing to apply for funding and for marketing itself as an organization that is independent of the EU helps the NGO to construct an image of itself as a neutral, depoliticized organization. In this regard, the antagonistic stance on EU funding is helpful.

Finally, a small gay, lesbian, bisexual and transsexual (GLBT) organization based in Istanbul expressed a similar, antagonistic strategy towards EU funding. The reasons for this were twofold. First, the NGO remained uncertain over how the government and the justice system viewed their activities. At the time of the interview, there was a widely publicized court case where an Istanbul municipality was trying to close down a GLBT NGO on the grounds that their actions were 'against morality'. These accusations echoed a similar, unsuccessful court case that some years ago had been brought against another GLBT NGO based in Ankara. Given this unfortunate lack of clarity on the legality of their activities, the organizations had a policy of not working on donor-funded projects. Additionally, the NGO was very clear that it did not want to become an organization that was purely focused on completing projects. This would contradict its status and identity as a grass-roots organization that was run on a volunteer basis. In effect the NGO was run by its members, for its members. Projects would divert attention away from these principles and towards external priorities introduced by the project. Where the NGO had a plan for some new work it wished to undertake, it would try to raise the necessary funds by organizing a fundraising event, not by applying for external funds. Resistance to EU funding is not absolute, for under the right circumstances they would consider EU funding; yet this represented a risk. There was a concern that projects would take over the agenda by requiring a shift away from the grass-roots focus and from the ad hoc way in which the NGO wanted to approach their work.[14]

The antagonistic responses to EU funding can be found across a wide spectrum of NGOs. In various areas of civil society – from Kemalist and

Islamist to GLBT NGOs, large and small – the antagonistic attitudes towards EU-funded projects surface in several different degrees of intensity. In each case, the antagonistic reaction offers something positive to the NGO. It can be a way of establishing a clearer sense of organizational purpose and objectives and help to bolster organizational identity by defining what the NGO is not. In this sense, this behaviour can be understood as protecting the independence of the NGO. For some, this antagonistic behaviour forms part of a broader suspicion and weariness towards the Europeanization project in Turkey. For others, it is a way of reaffirming the reasons for the NGO's existence; it is focused on particular issues, and the lure of project funding must not direct away from these issues.

Box 7.1   Summary of the four categories for NGO roles

Translator:	**Broker:**
NGOs seek to find ways to reconcile the ideas behind donor-funded projects in locally meaningful ways. They do so by reinterpreting the solutions offered by EU policy on the basis of their own interests and understanding.	NGOs act as entrepreneurial agents that facilitate links between donors and local actors. They do so by identifying the gaps that exist between EU projects and local NGOs and offering to bridge this gap.
Navigator:	**Antagonist:**
NGOs exhibit a similar entrepreneurial spirit as 'brokers' but utilize it in outcomes aimed at the NGO itself. They do so by identifying opportunities within the EU-funding framework and finding innovative ways to gain access to this funding.	NGOs refuse to accept EU funding or any other donor funding. They do so not only by avoiding EU funding but doing so publicly in order to garner support from those who share their scepticism.

It is challenging to offer an accurate assessment of the relative significance of each of these categories in the context of Turkish civil society and within the particular group of NGOs researched here. It is important to note that no NGO may fit perfectly – and solely – within one of the four roles described here. In other words, the same women's NGO may at one time function as a broker between a rural women's NGO and the EU, while behaving like a navigator at a later date. Having said this, at least among those NGOs that were interviewed as part of this research project, navigator-like behaviour was most prevalent. Even where NGOs did not admit to being navigators themselves, anecdotally almost every respondent referred to at least one example of another NGO that behaved in this way. This finding should not be surprising, considering the weak traditions of giving in Turkey discussed in Chapter 6, and the fact that NGOs are largely a recent phenomenon that have come to exist in an environment where external funding is a large motivating factor behind NGO activities. Additionally, the role of a translator or a broker requires a degree of specialist knowledge, which limits the number of NGOs able to carry out these roles.

Conclusion

As NGOs make decisions about how to negotiate a path through the contradictions that exist between their daily practices and the requirements of the EU-funding process, they generate new strategies that aim to reconcile the current position of the NGO with the prospect of funding opportunities. The strategies fall under two types. The first relates to the roles NGOs have as intermediaries, drawing on the model of NGOs as brokers and translators offered by David Lewis and David Mosse (2006). The second type focuses in on the direct relationship between NGOs and EU funding, explaining how NGOs position themselves in relation to the funding opportunities, as navigators and antagonists. While some find ways to navigate closer to EU funds by reframing their activities in opportunistic ways that grant them access, other NGOs find it beneficial to position themselves sternly against external funding.

The observations made in this chapter resonate strongly with the sociological institutionalist perspective of Europeanization that was discussed in Chapter 2. Donors that fund project-based interventions tend to see projects through a rational lens, favouring them because they are time-bound, technical interventions that lend themselves to the development of quantifiable outcomes and performance indicators. The actor-oriented perspective questions the rational assumptions that drive the aforesaid conception, pointing, for example, to the complex social processes of internalization that need to take place before projects become meaningful to local actors. It resonates with the sociological argument that places its focus on the local values and norms as key factors explaining local responses to externally derived goals. The rational and actor-oriented discussion of the project aims to add a layer of analysis to the theoretical approach developed earlier.

The strategies NGOs adopt may be in part based on rational calculations, but a crucial part of the equation hinges on the decisions NGOs make on the basis of their perception of the social context. The decisions NGOs make vis-à-vis EU funding are reflective of broader questions than simple utility-maximizing calculus of rational choice institutionalism. The four NGO roles outlined in this chapter offer an insight into the processes through which EU policy becomes socialized, and give a brief look at the way NGOs internalize the EU rules and norms in a variety of ways and how this process in turn leads EU policy to reach multiple outcomes rather than a single one.

The role of the CFCU reinforces the discrepancies between the donor world and the NGO world. Given the processes through which the CFCU assessed NGO performance and the requirements that are placed on NGOs, it is likely that the two lifeworlds of EU funding and NGOs are likely to remain disconnected. It seems that this disconnect has only widened after the CFCU assumed its role at the centre of the EU–NGO funding relationship. This trend therefore suggests that the pre-accession process, by sustaining and widening the EU–NGO gap, creates further incentives and reasons for NGOs to engage in the roles of translators, brokers, navigators and antagonists.

The chapter demonstrates the multidimensionality of donor–NGO relations. While actor-oriented networks highlight the inadvertent consequences of donor-funded projects, any analysis within the actor-oriented framework is tightly focused on the social interface that a project creates. By illustrating the various roles NGOs engage in, and particularly the various motivations that underlie these roles, the discussion has attempted to push beyond that which takes place around projects themselves and highlight the multidimensionality and unpredictability of the impact that EU funding can have on Turkish civil society. The impact of EU funding spills over from the contained project sphere, and points to the difficulties in predicting the outcome of donor policy. The unintended side effects suggest that policy interventions, such as democracy promotion through NGO funding, cannot be thought of as simply executing a plan of action that has expected outcomes. To gain a better understanding of the true impact of EU pre-accession policy it is necessary to look more holistically at how NGOs engage with and react to EU policy, and how they embrace, adapt or resist this policy depending on their interests.

The consequences of social action are rarely restricted to the specific policy area for which they were intended. We should remain wary of project aims that are based on a simple execution of a predefined plan with expected outcomes. The intermediary actors that operate at the junction where the donor worldview links up with the Turkish worldview are but one example of the myriad actors that contribute to the unexpected and nuanced outcomes of donor funding. This invites one to question whether the outcomes of EU-funded projects have actually been different from what was planned. The evidence from this chapter suggests that if the project outcomes are premised on NGO projects reaching particular end results (as evidence from Chapter 3 suggests), then, given how the EU funding to civil society is unfolding, any specific outcomes are unlikely to materialize. Where the policy aspirations are not congruent with the NGOs' own goals, the organizations are skilled in finding ways in which to circumvent the aspirations donors have for NGO activities.

8
Conclusion

The EU accession negotiations, by their very nature, crystallize around processes of change. These processes ask Turkey to accept a set of rules and norms that require wide-ranging internal adaptations, and which largely determine the official role that civil society funding plays in the accession context. In other words, the EU rationale for civil society funding links to a perception of NGOs as potential agents of domestic change. The research presented here has asked how EU policy on civil society expects NGOs to deliver change, and identified a conceptual frame for describing these expectations in democratization and Europeanization. The EU anticipates that Turkish civil society can contribute to the accession process by further democratizing and Europeanizing Turkey.

A central aim of this book has been to explore the unpredictability of the Europeanization processes that are attached to EU civil society funding in Turkey and identified a disconnect between the EU policy framework and NGO behaviour as a key course of this unpredictability. This disconnect was investigated from a number of points of view. The dominance of liberal individualism and liberal democratic ideas among donors and policymakers is offered as a partial explanation. The Western tradition of thought in relation to civil society contains a strong tendency to draw links between the existence of a vibrant civil society, processes of democratization and improved policy efficiency. In other words, civil society is seen as a source of 'good'. This approach also permeates initiatives that deal with civil society in the EU enlargement context: the rationale for engaging with NGOs in Turkey is linked to democratization and improved dialogue between EU countries and Turkey. The book has argued that the transposition of civil society-related policies from the EU domestic context to the enlargement context suggests a universal understanding of what is meant by civil society and NGOs. Furthermore, as both of these goals – democratization and improved dialogue – are deemed to be core conditions for Turkey's EU accession, the role envisaged for NGOs is instrumental in nature. Following this line of argument, the chapters suggested that NGO work is valued for the contribution it makes to the broader processes of democratization and Europeanization.

Moreover, the book has put forward a case for the importance of understanding the Turkish socio-cultural and historical context as a key determinant of NGO behaviour. The essentialized character of NGO activity that follows on from the historical development of civil society in Turkey means that NGOs are reluctant to cooperate and work together, and they tend to be sensitive to polarization along the lines of politics or identity (secular–religious cleavages being explored in some detail in the thesis). Given that this politically charged context is often intermingled with passionate nationalist and secular tendencies, EU funding (along with other external interventions) is rejected on the grounds that it constitutes an agenda for trying to surreptitiously influence domestic policy and politics. Additionally, NGOs that do not subscribe to such scepticism often felt that EU funding is either unfair in terms of accessibility, remaining unreachable to many organizations, or contains monitoring criteria that are far too complicated. These kinds of attitudes among NGO activists contribute to the unpredictability of EU policy because the policy assumes engagement with, and embracement of, what it represents. Yet many, perhaps a majority of NGOs, refuse to accept EU policy at face value and manoeuvre in ways that reconcile their own goals with those of the EU. The opportunities for such manoeuvres emerge precisely because a gap is present between policy aspirations of the EU and reality on the ground. This agency that NGOs exhibit in their activities was identified as a key explanatory factor for the presence of unpredictability in the processes of Europeanization and democratization.

Chapter 2 outlined social change as a central idea that has informed the way in which Western societies have come to think about civil society. Thinkers such as Ferguson, Hegel and de Tocqueville strove to make sense of the new kinds of social relations that were presented to them by a modernizing and industrializing world. The concept of civil society was interwoven with a changing society, and such ideas continue to inform thinking on civil society, with democratization and sustainable economic development emerging as the key motivations for this. In the EU policy lexicon in particular, the notion of a third sector brings together both the democratic and economic benefits of civil society and wraps the argument in the idea that civil society contributes to change and to a societal forward motion. The chapter found that the relevance of such concepts in the Turkish context is well worth reviewing because the third sector approach presents an overly positive and uniform view of the way civil society likely relates to change. Any overall picture of civil society activity is likely to be confused and multidirectional, reflecting the countless opinions and positions that various actors express, in turn alluding to the need for a contextually grounded understanding of civil society.

Chapter 3 carried the discussion forward to the EU policy on civil society and explored how the aims of democratization and Europeanization become expressed in this policy. The chapter put forward two broad findings. First, a discursive shift away from democratization and towards Europeanization was identified. By 2003 the policy discussions on the role of civil society had become intricately linked with the process of EU enlargement and the accession process. EU policy has approached civil society not only as an element of liberal democracy with an essential role in the expression of human rights and citizenship, but also utilized it in a parallel discourse of what it takes for accession countries to become Europeanized more broadly. Second, the chapter suggested that the belief in the ability of civil society to contribute to the democratization and Europeanization processes depends on particular assumptions about NGO behaviour. One such assumption views NGOs from a *universal perspective*, whereby they are deemed to operate in similar ways in different contexts. Another assumption views NGOs from an *instrumental perspective*, seeing organizations as neutral vehicles to be used for the delivery of policies and to perform particular functions. Moreover, the chapter alluded to similar observations with regard to EU civil society policy both in the Mediterranean region and in Turkey, further confirming the instrumental and universal nature of EU policy.

In the Mediterranean, EU policy has focused primarily on human rights and democracy. However, in Turkey since the start of the accession negotiations, there has been a more decisive shift away from policies that support civil society in direct democratization efforts, towards softer and less confrontational policies of Europeanization (adopting the *acquis communautaire* of the EU).

Chapter 4, the bridge to the empirical chapters that follow, provided the contextual flesh around the theoretical and policy discussions by considering the history and development of civil society in Turkey. The processes of Westernization and modernization that were set in motion in the 1920s and 1930s, together with aspirations for a modern, Western nation state, provided an important impetus for the present-day processes of Europeanization. On the one hand, Europeanization has generated the context – an enabling environment – within which NGOs are able to carry out their work. On the other hand, NGOs are an integral part of the Europeanization process. The particular way in which Westernization and modernization turned out in Turkey also present limitations to the way in which Europeanization can now unfold. The aspirations for reform, for example, are complicated by the domestic political context, where the secular and Islamic camps in particular are engaged in a hegemonic struggle over the political direction of the country. The essential nature of the debate that surrounds this issue, together with the fact that NGOs tend to take sides in this essentialist debate, contribute to the fragmented political discourse as well as to fragmentation within civil society. The policies that are part of the EU accession process become inevitably entangled in these debates, the chapter argued, complicating the processes of societal Europeanization in particular.

Chapter 5, the first of the three empirical chapters, explored the impact of EU funding on the relationships that Turkish advocacy NGOs are able to establish with governmental actors as well as with other NGOs. NGO advocacy, being largely about aspirations for change, resonates strongly with the change processes related to EU accession. The impact of EU accession has been most profound at the level of legal changes that have significantly bolstered NGO efforts at advocacy. However, where the EU has financed projects aiming to improve relations between advocacy NGOs and municipal governments, these have had limited success, highlighting the need for such relationships to develop organically from within. Developing them with the help of external funding is unlikely to yield the results that were expected. Relationships between advocacy NGOs are often beleaguered by political or ideological debates and tensions, which get in the way of working together or focusing on the issues in a way that is productive and could contribute positively to the policy agenda. The chapter thus suggested that the Turkish context imposes limitations to the ability of NGOs to collaborate in ways that would be directly relevant to the effectiveness of government policy. This in turn has cast a question mark over EU policies that envisage such roles for NGOs.

Chapter 6 queried the appropriateness of EU funding by looking at how appropriate it has been in relation to domestic avenues for funding and how it has shaped NGO responses to external funding. The domestic funding environment is rather unfavourable for advocacy NGOs, which tend not to be supported through domestic philanthropic endeavours. In this sense EU funding offers a good fit, as it has tended to channel its support to those NGOs that would not otherwise have many domestic opportunities available to them. Since the start of the EU accession negotiations, the mechanics of the funding process have been Europeanized, introducing further bureaucratic complexity. Two domestic institutions, the CFCU and CSDC have effectively been tasked with moulding the funded NGOs into vehicles for delivering EU policy goals. Two issues internal to NGOs emerged as determinants of NGO participation in EU-funded projects. Firstly, NGOs felt that only those organizations with a certain internal organizational capacity were able to successfully bid for projects. Secondly, NGOs made decisions on whether to apply for EU funding on the basis of where the NGO perceived the legitimacy of their operations to come from. Some groups made explicit choices not to apply for funding, as they believe that EU funding labels them as less genuine or organic as a Turkish NGO. These inadvertent selection processes bifurcate civil society into 'haves and have-nots' or the 'wants and want-nots'. The chapter concluded that these developments imposed limits as to how far-reaching and ambitious EU aims of building civil society through project funding can be.

Chapter 7 carried on the discussion with regard to the choices that NGOs make. The debate was harnessed by a focus on the notion of the project. The project interface through which EU funding is channelled to NGOs is not a closed box where actions can be controlled by the performance criteria assigned to the project. The chapter suggested that the incongruence between policy expectations and everyday practices among NGOs mean that organizations generate a variety of means to negotiate through these differences in ways that are beneficial to them. These strategies were labelled as 'brokers', 'translators', 'navigators' and 'antagonists'. Such actions allude to the unanticipated consequences that are generated by the EU policy process. It is therefore less certain that EU civil society funding will achieve any specific policy aims it sets out. The outcomes are likely to be more fuzzy, varied and uncertain.

The research also pointed to certain differences in how the findings related to the different regional sites where interviews were conducted. While findings from Ankara and Istanbul yielded similar results, the experiences of interviewees from Diyarbakir were somewhat different. In Diyarbakir NGO actors exhibited a more open attitude towards cooperation with other organizations – arguably because all the NGOs deal with the consequences of the years of unrest the region has experienced: there is a shared feeling that everyone is in the same boat. The interviewees also felt that EU funding had a stronger impact in the southeast of Turkey. As a region it is much poorer than the other two research sites, which in turn has meant that smaller amounts of EU financial assistance are able to make more of a difference in people's lives. Such differences between the research sites suggested that regions are an important variable to consider. However, it was not within the scope of this research project to do so, as more comparative work to substantiate any findings would have been required.

The account of NGO behaviour that is put forward in this book is not one that is strictly limited to Turkey. During the previous rounds of EU enlargement, and indeed among older EU member states, NGOs have exhibited similar tendencies to come up with creative ways in which to resist the demands for change that EU civil society funding places on them. However, the book does suggest that there is a particular Turkish narrative for explaining why NGOs behave the way they do, and that this narrative forms an important part of an analysis of Turkish civil society.

The broader picture

The conclusions in this book also aim to make a contribution to a number of broader discussions that concern the role of civil society in bringing about social change and the means by which civil society is engaged in these change processes. First, the dynamics of civil society activity in Turkey supports a Hegelian interpretation of civil society as a site of struggle and contest, where particular interests are in constant competition with other particular interests. Second, the Turkish case evokes a Gramscian analysis, where hegemonic and counterhegemonic voices challenge each other's legitimacy in a public debate. This is largely conducted through an essentialized debate, where the voices are engaged in an uncompromising mission to convert the other to see the wrongs of their way. It is not merely different particular interests that are jostling for position, but rather different versions of the universal interests that are battling for the heart of the state.

Third, EU civil society policy in Turkey is heavily influenced by a third sector perspective, a political economy approach that emphasizes the efficiency gains and increased effectiveness greater civil society involvement can bring to policy design and delivery. However, this technical approach fits rather awkwardly on top of Turkish civil society that is highly charged both politically and ideologically. As the latter chapters of the book demonstrate, the incentives that are built into EU policy measures to induce certain type of behaviour are easily side-stepped by a desire to engage in a particular type of political or ideological activism. Fourth, this incongruence of the rational–logical approach evident in EU policy and the way Turkish civil society actors operate on the ground suggests that we need to understand Europeanization in a particular way. The framework of sociological institutionalism gives us a way to understand this incongruence and to make sense of the way in which civil society responses to EU civil society policy manifest themselves. It is by appreciating the influence of the social context in which NGOs operate and the informal rules and norms that govern their behaviour that we can understand how EU civil society policy becomes socialized by NGOs and becomes meaningful in the local context.

These observations lead us to think about the means by which civil society actors are enlisted to take forward the EU policy agenda. Policy can be an effective catalyst for change as policies encapsulate a certain way of behaving that shapes actors' understanding of the role they are to play. Policy that induces change, however, is also likely to be met with uncertainty. The preceding chapters have documented several examples of the tensions that arise from the disconnections between what is proposed and the current state of affairs, creating a vast range of reactions among NGOs engaged in the policy process. The NGO reactions are embedded in the domestic political context that is also employed to interpret the meaning of EU policy based on local interpretations. These interpretations become highly relevant when we look at the primary means through which funding is made available: projects. The monitoring mechanisms that accompany project funding in particular can compound the feeling among recipients that the EU aims to control civil society in Turkey. Projects as time-bound activities are focused on a fixed set of outcomes rather than thinking about the process through which the project is realized, and what implications this has on the sustainability of the defined outcomes beyond the lifecycle of the project. It seems the latter makes for a more appropriate measure of real social change.

There is indeed evidence that EU civil society policy is able to induce certain types of changes. Yet any such impact is rather ambivalent and uncertain in nature. Funding has shaped civil society in a certain direction, creating winners and losers on the bases of organizational ability and orientation; by offering encouragement to certain types of organizations, the policy has amounted to a transformative process. At the same time, policy that induces change also generates uncertain outcomes. EU policies have a sense of being imposed from above, leading to strategies of resistance and deviance on the part of local actors.

The book has highlighted the uncertainty and ambiguity that is evident in the outcomes of EU funding; but where exactly does this leave us in terms of moving forward? Has the EU either adopted wrong aims or wrong policies to achieve said aims? In the context of the EU pre-accession process that Turkey has embarked on, this does not seem a plausible argument to make. Certain steps need to be taken for Turkey to continue its journey towards an eventual membership, and the nature of civil society funding is one aspect of that process. However, what exactly is achievable through this funding needs to be given some further thought. Processes of Europeanization or democratization are not simple behavioural traits that can be adopted overnight. They are long-term processes that evolve incrementally and will inevitably look different in each country context. In order to ensure that the NGOs are fully involved and share the policy aims, they should be included in the decision-making processes that form a part of the annual review of policy priorities.

If the EU continues to present itself as a benevolent but inflexible bureaucratic behemoth, in the eyes of the NGOs it may not differ so much from the state whose traditions it is trying to change. It would therefore be more prudent to focus on processes, rather than short-term outcomes. Whether a given project lives up to the stated aims is less important than ensuring the aims are arrived at through a participatory process. By including NGOs at all stages of decision-making, they are likely to gain a much stronger sense of ownership over the policies and projects that they are asked to act upon. This means that the EU will have to compromise on some of its aims in order to facilitate a genuine dialogue; but given the current uncertainty of policy outcomes, this would be a positive step for all considered.

Notes

1   Introduction

1. The term 'NGO' refers to a particular subset of civil society organizations that engages in advocacy activities. The term 'civil society organization' (CSO) is in turn used to refer to the totality of organizational forms that exists in civil society. The purpose of this distinction is to draw a line between CSOs that refer to the totality of organizations found within civil society and NGOs as particular organizations that form the focus of the research: professional advocacy NGOs working on rights-based issues.
2. This term refers to the total body of European law each member state is required to accept as a condition of EU membership.
3. The other two approaches are 'rational choice institutionalism' and 'historical institutionalism'. Rational choice institutionalism assumes that actors have fixed preferences and always employ strategies that aim to maximize self-interest. It emphasizes the role of major EU institutions, such as the European Commission and European Parliament, as the structuring agents between other actors. Historical institutionalism considers the short- and long-term impact of institutions. It agrees on the initial premise of rational choice institutionalism – that institutions and actors are bound in a strategic game of interest bargaining – but foresees the development of path dependencies in the long term. That is, institutional ways of behaving, or cultures, develop that constrict the strategic choices available to actors under rational choice institutionalism. This is not to say these approaches hold no explanatory power, yet they remain less relevant to the type of empirical task at hand here (Kazamias and Featherstone, 2001, pp. 7–9).

2   Europeanization from a Civil Society Perspective

1. See, for example, the contributions found in Keane (1988).
2. The analysis offered here is intended as a preamble to Chapter 4 which is focused entirely on elaborating the case of Turkey.

3   EU Civil Society Policy

1. See Chapter 7 for a more detailed consideration of the critique offered by Ferguson, Long and others.
2. MEDA stands for *mesure d'ajustement* and is the 'legal framework for the bulk of EU aid to Mediterranean Partner Countries across a wide range of sectors' (Stetter, 2003).

3. The countries considered under EU's Mediterranean policy are Algeria, Egypt, Israel, Jordan, Lebanon, Morocco, Occupied Palestinian Territory, Syria, Tunisia and Turkey (on certain occasions, unless a country-specific policy exists as part of the pre-accession process).
4. See *Euro-Mediterranean Partnership, Regional Co-operation – An Overview of Programmes and Projects* (2007) for more detail. There are other programmes such as 'Med-Pact – Local Authorities', which aim to encourage dialogue and cooperation between cities and civil societies, and in so doing push for a greater 'cultural and social rapprochement between the EU and the Mediterranean partners' (Med-Pact, 2009), and the 'EuroMed Civil Forum', which aspires to create a platform through which to 'strengthen the role of civil society organisations in the region' by being able to 'network, discuss [NGOs'] role, and make recommendations to governments' (European Commission, 2007a, p. 70).
5. Interview with a senior civil servant, EU delegation to Turkey, Ankara, 3 April 2008.

4 Civil Society in Turkey

1. By comparison, French women achieved these same rights in 1944 and Italians in 1946, while the Swiss women were given the right to vote in federal elections only in 1971.
2. Also translated as the 'Confederation of Progressive Trade Unions of Turkey'.
3. For a discussion of how this distinction between 'civil' and 'non-military' affects Turkish definitions of 'civil society' (*sivil toplum*), see Seckinelgin (2004).
4. The organizations involved included the Turkish Union of Chambers and Commodities Exchanges (TOBB), the Turkish Industrialists' and Businessmen's Association (TÜSİAD), the Economic Development Foundation (İKV), the Turkish Union of Agricultural Chambers (TZOB), TÜRK-İŞ, Turkish Confederation of Employers' Unions (TİSK), the Confederation of Public Servants' Union (MEMUR-SEN) and the Television Broadcasters' Association (TVYD).

5 NGO Relationships

1. This section is based on an interview with a senior civil servant at the Directorate of Acts and Resolutions, Turkish Parliament, Ankara, 27 June 2008.
2. Ibid.
3. The point of view put forth in this paragraph reflects the official government position, as expressed in an interview with Dr Şentürk Uzun, the Head of the DoA, Ankara, 8 August 2007.
4. Interview with Dr Şentürk Uzun, the Head of the DoA, Ankara, 8 August 2007.

5. Interview with a senior EU civil servant, EU Delegation to Turkey, Ankara, 3 April 2008.
6. Interview with an Islamic women's activist, Istanbul, 14 April 2008.
7. Representing Kurdish interests, DEHAP was a reincarnation of the People's Democracy Party (HADEP). HADEP was banned in 2003 on the grounds that it supported the terrorist activities of the Kurdistan Workers Party (PKK). In 2005, the new DEHAP merged to form the Democratic Society Party (DTP). In December 2009 DTP was shut down on 'charges of ethnic separatism' (*Today's Zaman*, 2009).
8. Interview with a member of a Muslim human rights NGO, Diyarbakir, 1 July 2008 and with a member of a women's NGO, Diyarbakir, 2 July 2008.
9. Interview with a member of a women's NGO, Diyarbakir, 2 July 2008.
10. Interview with a member of a women's NGO, Istanbul, 6 April 2008.
11. Interview with a senior EU civil servant, EU Delegation to Turkey, Ankara, 3 April 2008.
12. This account is based entirely on the interview with the director of the children's NGO and may not offer a full picture. When I raised the issue during subsequent interviews with representatives of the CFCU, who should have been responsible for the financial oversight of the project, nobody, due to staffing changes, was able to recall that such a project had ever existed. The website for the project www.skip.tr.org has been decommissioned at least since January 2008, which is when I first tried to access it.
13. Interview with the director of a child-rights NGO, Ankara, 2 April 2008.
14. Adam Fagan (2010) 'Civil Society Assistance or State-Building? Evaluating Donor Assistance in Bosnia–Herzegovina and Serbia'. Paper read at the *For Better or Worse? Civil Society and Transitions in the Western Balkans* workshop, London School of Economics, 7 May.
15. This opinion draws on the following interviews: interviews with a female activist, Ankara, 1 April 2008; a member of a women's NGO, Ankara, 8 August 2007; a women's rights activist, Istanbul, 15 August 2007; and a member of a women's NGO, Ankara, 1 April 2008.
16. Interview with a member of a women's NGO, Ankara, 1 April 2008.
17. Interview with a member of a women's NGO, Ankara, 3 April 2008.
18. Interview with a female activist, Istanbul, 24 June 2008.
19. Interview with a female activist, Ankara, 1 April 2008.
20. Interview with a member of a women's NGO, Ankara, 3 April 2008.
21. Interview with a member of a women's NGO, Istanbul, 14 April 2008.

6   Civil Society Support in Turkey

1. Interview with a representative of the Friedrich Naumann Foundation, Istanbul, 3 July 2008.
2. Interview with a representative of the Finnish Embassy in Turkey, Ankara, 4 April 2008.

3. The CIVICUS Civil Society Index reports are compiled by CSOs at the country level that offer an assessment of the current state of civil society by employing the 'Diamond Tool' developed by Helmut Anheier. This is a four-dimensional assessment of the 'health' of civil society based on the criteria of 'structure', 'values', 'environment' and 'impact' (CIVICUS, 2010; TUSEV, 2005).

4. In recent years this practice has been challenged as some municipalities have allowed religious organizations to arrange such collections.

5. Interview with a women's rights activist, Istanbul, 15 August 2007.

6. Interview with the director of a human rights NGO, Istanbul, 24 June 2008.

7. Interview with a women's rights activist, Istanbul, 15 August 2007.

8. This section is largely based on an interview with a senior EU civil servant, EU Delegation to Turkey, Ankara, 3 April 2008.

9. Ibid.

10. Ibid.

11. Interview with senior EU civil servant, EU Delegation to Turkey, Ankara, 3 April 2008.

12. Interview with the director of CFCU, 27 June 2008.

13. Interview with a member of a women's NGO, Ankara, 1 April 2008.

14. Interview with the director of the CSDC, Ankara, 7 August 2008.

15. Interview with a member of a women's NGO, Ankara, 14 April 2008.

16. Interview with a member of a youth NGO, Istanbul, 4 July 2008.

17. I received copies of such EU-funded reports on honour killings from no less than three different women's NGOs during my fieldwork.

18. Interview with a member of a youth NGO, Ankara, 6 August 2007.

19. Interview with a member of a women's NGO, Istanbul, 6 April 2008.

20. Interview with a member of a women's NGO, Ankara, 1 April 2008.

21. Interview with a member of a youth NGO, Ankara, 6 August 2007.

22. Interview with a member of a women's NGO, Istanbul, 6 April 2008.

23. Interview with a member of a women's NGO, Istanbul, 16 August 2008.

24. Interview with a member of an Islamic women's NGO, Ankara, 8 August 2007.

25. Interview with a member of a women's NGO, Diyarbakir, 1 July 2008.

26. Interview with a member of a women's NGO, Ankara, 3 April 2008.

27. Interview with a member of Muslim human rights NGO, Diyarbakir, 1 July 2008.

28. Interview with a member of a youth NGO, Istanbul, 4 July 2008.

29. Interview with a member of a women's NGO in Ankara, 8 August 2007.

30. Interview with Dr Yoruk Kurtaran from the Youth Studies Centre at Bilgi University, Istanbul, 3 July 2008.

31. Interview with a member of a youth foundation, Istanbul, 14 August 2008.

32. Interview with a youth activist, Ankara, 6 August 2008.

33. Interview with a member of a women's NGO, Ankara, 1 April 2008.

34. Interview with a women's NGO activist, Istanbul, 6 April 2008.

7   Tracing the Impact of EU Policy on the Ground

1. See the third section for a more detailed discussion of the Paris Declaration.
2. The information in this section is based on interviews conducted with two representatives of the CFCU in Ankara, 26 and 27 June 2008.
3. This analysis is based on the written minutes of the of the two meetings (CSDC, 2005, 2006).
4. Interview with Dr Şentürk Uzun, the Head of the DoA, Ankara, 8 August 2007.
5. Interview with the director of CFCU, Ankara, 27 June 2008.
6. Interview with a senior EU civil servant, EU Delegation in Turkey, Ankara, 3 April 2007.
7. Interview with the director of CSDC, Ankara, 7 August 2007.
8. Ibid.
9. Interview with the director of a human rights NGO, Istanbul, 24 June 2008.
10. As a consequence of Turkish government policy in the Kurdish region, between 378,335 (official government figure) and three million (estimation by Turkish NGO, Human Rights Association) people have been forced to leave their homes (Çelik, 2005). A vast majority of these people have congregated in Diyarbakir (http://www.hips.hacettepe.edu.tr/eng/tgyona_eng.shtml).
11. Interview with a member of a women's NGO, Diyarbakir, 2 July 2008.
12. Interview with a member of a women's NGO, Ankara, 3 April 2008.
13. Interview with a member of a human rights NGO, Diyarbakir, 1 July 2008.
14. Interview with a member of a GLBT NGO, Istanbul, 7 April 2008.

Bibliography

Aktar, Cengiz (2007) 'The Vaudeville around Article 301'. *Turkish Daily News*, 13 February.

Anheier, Helmut K. and Wolfgang Seibel (1989) *The third sector: Comparative studies of nonprofit organizations*. Berlin: de Gruyter.

Anıl, Ela, Canan Arın, Ayfle Berktay Hacımırzaoğlu, Mehveş Bingöllü, Pınar Ilkkaracan and Liz Ercevik Amado (2005) *Turkish civil and penal code reforms from a gender perspective: The success of two nationwide campaigns*. Istanbul: WWHR – New Ways.

Aras, Bülent and Ömer Caha (2000) 'Fethullah Gülen and his liberal "Turkish Islam" movement'. *Middle East Review of International Affairs* 4(4): 31–42.

Ayata, Ayşe Güneş and Fatma Tütüncü (2008) 'Party politics of the AKP (2002–2007) and the predicaments of women at the intersection of the Westernist, Islamist and feminist discourses in Turkey'. *British Journal of Middle Eastern Studies* 35(3): 363–84.

Bebbington, Anthony, Samuel Hickey and Diana Mitlin, eds (2008) *Can NGOs make a difference? The challenge of development alternatives*. London: Zed Books.

Blind, Peride Kaleağasi (2007) 'A new actor in Turkish democratization: Labor unions'. *Turkish Studies* 8(2): 289–311.

Brandtner, Barbara and Allan Rosas (1998) 'Human rights and the external relations of the European community: An analysis of doctrine and practice'. *European Journal of International Law* 9(3): 468–90.

Bratton, Michael (1989) 'The politics of government–NGO relations in Africa'. *World Development* 17(4): 569–87.

Carkoğlu, Ali (2006) 'Trends in individual giving and foundation practices in Turkey', in Filiz Bikmen and Rana Zincir, eds. *Philanthropy in Turkey: Citizens, foundations and the pursuit of social justice*. Istanbul: TUSEV, pp. 95–102.

Carothers, Thomas (1997) 'Democracy assistance: The question of strategy'. *Democratization* 4(3): 109–32.

—— (1999) *Aiding democracy abroad: The learning curve*. Washington, DC: Carnegie Endowment for International Peace.

—— (2004) *Critical mission: Essays on democracy promotion*. Washington, DC: Carnegie Endowment for International Peace.

Çelik, Ayşe Betül (2005) 'Transnationalization of human rights norms and its impact on internally displaced Kurds'. *Human Rights Quarterly* 27: 969–97.

CFCU (2009) *Central Finance and Contracts Unit*. Available from http://www.cfcu.gov.tr/about.php?lng=en&action=cfcu. Accessed on 3 November 2009.

Chandhoke, Neera (1995) *State and civil society: Explorations in political theory*. New Delhi; Thousand Oaks, CA: Sage Publications.

—— (2001) 'The "civil" and the "political" in civil society'. *Democratization* 8(2): 1–24.

—— (2007) 'Civil society'. *Development in Practice* 17(4): 607–14.

CIVICUS (2010) *CIVICUS Civil Society Index Report: Background.* Available from http://www.civicus.org/csi/csi-background. Accessed on 2 July 2010.

Civil Society Dialogue Project (2009) *What is the Civil Society Dialogue Project*, 12 January. Available from http://www.csdproject.net/web/AboutTheProgramme/tabid/54/language/en-US/Default.aspx. Accessed on 10 June 2009.

Clark, John D. (2010) 'Advocacy', in Helmut Anheier, Stefan Toepler and Regina List, eds. *International encyclopedia of civil society.* New York: Springer, pp. 12–18.

Communities and Local Government (2008) *Communities in control: Real people, real power.* Norwich: The Stationary Office.

Crawford, Gordon (1997) 'Foreign aid and political conditionality: Issues of effectiveness and consistency'. *Democratization* 4(3): 69–108.

—— (1998) 'Human rights and democracy in EU development co-operation: Towards fair and equal treatment', in Marjorie Lister, ed. *European Union development policy.* Houndmills: MacMillan Press, pp. 131–78.

—— (2001) 'Evaluating EU promotion of human rights, democracy and good governance: Towards a participatory approach'. *European Development Policy Study Group.* Available from http://www.edpsg.org/Documents/Dp22.doc. Accessed on 15 December 2010.

—— (2007) 'EU and democracy promotion in Africa: High on rhetoric, low on delivery?' in Andrew Mold, ed. *EU development policy in a changing world: Challenges for the 21st century.* Amsterdam: Amsterdam University Press, pp. 169–97.

Crowley, Jocelyn Elise, Margaret Watson and Maureen R. Waller (2008) 'Understanding: Language, public policy, and democracy'. *Perspectives on Politics* 6(1): 71–88.

CSDC (2005) *Outcomes of the 1st Meeting of the Advisory Board.* Available from http://www.stgm.org/docs/1158914638STGMAdvisoryCommiteeMeeting Report–30%2009%202005Eng.doc. Accessed on 22 May 2007.

—— (2006) *Outcomes of the 2nd Advisory Board Meeting.* Available from http://www.stgm.org/docs/1158930730danismakurulueng.doc. Accessed 22 May 2007.

De Tocqueville, Alexis (1998) *Democracy in America.* London: Penguin.

De Zeeuw, Jeroen (2005) 'Projects do not create institutions: The record of democracy assistance in post-conflict societies'. *Democratization* 12(4): 481–504.

DFID (2009) *The Paris Declaration on Aid Effectiveness and Accra Agenda for Action.* Available from http://www.dfid.gov.uk/Global-Issues/Working-to-make-Global-Aid-more-effective/The-Paris-Declaration-on-Aid-Effectiveness-and-Accra-Agenda-for-Action-/. Accessed on 27 February 2010.

Diamond, L. (1994) 'Rethinking civil society: Toward democratic consolidation'. *Journal of Democracy* 5(3): 4–17.

Diez, Thomas (1999) 'Speaking "Europe": The politics of integration discourse'. *Journal of European Public Policy* 6(4): 598–613.

Diez, Thomas, Apostolos Agnantopoulos and Alper Kaliber (2005) 'File: Turkey, Europeanization and civil society'. *South European Society and Politics* 10(1): 1–15.

Dodd, Chris (1992) 'The development of Turkish democracy'. *British Journal of Middle Eastern Studies* 19(1): 16–30.

Dryzek, John S. (1990) *Discursive democracy: Politics, policy, and science.* Cambridge: Cambridge University Press.

Eade, Deborah (2007) 'Capacity building: Who builds whose capacity?' *Development in Practice* 17(4–5): 630–9.

Edwards, Michael and David Hulme (1996) *Beyond the magic bullet: NGO performance and accountability in the post-Cold War world,* Kumarian Press books on international development. West Hartford, CO: Kumarian Press.

Eilstrup-Sangiovanni, Mette, ed. (2006) *Debates on European integration: A reader,* European Union series. Basingstoke; New York: Palgrave Macmillan.

Erdoğan, Necmi (2000) 'Kemalist non-governmental organizations: Troubled elites in defence of a sacred heritage', in Stefan Yerasimos, Günter Seufert and Karin Vorhoff, eds. *Civil society in the grip of nationalism.* Istanbul: Orient-Institut, pp. 251–82.

Etzioni, Amitai (1973) 'The third sector and domestic missions'. *Public Administration Review* 33(4): 314–23.

European Commission (1992) *An open and structured dialogue between the Commission and special interest groups.* Brussels: Commission of the European Communities.

—— (1997) *Communication from the Commission on Promoting the role of voluntary organisations and foundations in Europe.* Brussels: Commission of the European Communities.

—— (2000) Commission discussion paper. *The commission and non-governmental organizations: Building a stronger partnership.* Brussels: Commission of the European Communities.

—— (2001) *White paper European governance.* Brussels: Commission of the European Communities.

—— (2003a) *Report from the Commission on European Governance.* Luxembourg: Office for Official Publications.

—— (2003b) *Reinvigorating EU actions on human rights and democratization with Mediterranean partners – Strategic guidelines,* COM(2003) 294 final. Brussels: European Commission.

—— (2003c) *Improving co-operation between the NGOs and the public sector and strengthening the NGOs' democratic participation level.* TR0301.03.

—— (2004a) *Strengthening freedom of association for further development of civil society,* TR 04.01.04.

—— (2004b) *Recommendation of the European Commission on Turkey's progress towards accession,* COM(2004) 656. Brussels: Commission of the European Communities.

—— (2005) *Strengthening civil society in the pre-accession process: NGO Grant Facility*, TR 05 01.02.

—— (2006a) *Civil society dialogue – EU–Turkish Chambers Forum*, TR 06 04.03.

—— (2006b) *Promotion of the civil society dialogue between EU and TK*, TR 06 04 01.

—— (2006c) *Civil society dialogue – Bringing together workers from Turkey and European Union through a 'shared culture of work'*, TR 06 04.04.

—— (2007a) *Euro-Mediterranean partnership. Regional co-operation: An overview of programmes and projects*. Brussels: European Commission.

—— (2007b) EU Turkey Review. Available from http://www.avrupa.info.tr/Files/File/AB-Gorunum/Sayi-09/01%20REVIEW.pdf. Accessed on 11 March 2009.

—— (2008) *Barcelona process: Union for the Mediterranean*, 20/05/08 COM(2008) 319 (Final). Brussels: European Commission.

—— (2010a) *What is the EU funding for?* Available from http://www.avrupa.info.tr/AB_Mali_Destegi/Neden_Ab_Mali_Destegi.html. Accessed on 9 February 2010.

—— (2010b) *Ongoing projects in 2007*. Available from http://www.avrupa.info.tr/Files//ongoing_projects_in_2007.doc. Accessed on 9 February 2010.

European Union (2005) Communication from the Commission to the Council, the European Parliament, the European Economic and Social Committee and the Committee of the Regions – *Civil Society Dialogue between the EU and Candidate Countries*.

—— (2009) *Glossary: Accession criteria*. Available from http://europa.eu/scadplus/glossary/accession_criteria_copenhague_en.htm. Accessed on 15 January 2010.

EUSG (2009) *Youth Initiatives for Dialogue Grant Scheme*. Secretariat General for EU Affairs. Available from http://www.abgs.gov.tr/index.php?p=5970&l=2. Accessed on 19 June 2009.

Evin, Ahmet (1994) 'Demilitarization and civilianization of the regime', in Metin Heper and Ahmet Evin, eds. *Politics in the third Turkish republic*. Boulder, CO: Westview Press, pp. 23–40.

Ferguson, Adam (1995) *An essay on the history of civil society*, Cambridge texts in the history of political thought. New York: Cambridge University Press.

Ferguson, James (1990) *The anti-politics machine: 'Development,' depoliticization, and bureaucratic power in Lesotho*. Cambridge: Cambridge University Press.

Ferlie, Ewan, Kate McLaughlin and Stephen P. Osborne (2001) *New public management: Current trends and future prospects*. London: Routledge.

Finke, Barbara (2007) 'Civil society participation in EU governance'. *Living Reviews in European Governance* 2(2). Available from http://europeangovernance.livingreviews.org/Articles/lreg-2007-2/download/lreg-2007-2Color.pdf. Accessed on 18 October 2010.

Foresti, Marta, David Booth and Tammie O'Neil (2006) *Aid effectiveness and human rights: Strengthening the implementation of the Paris Declaration*. London: Overseas Development Institute.

Fowler, Alan (1997) *Striking a balance: A guide to enhancing the effectiveness of non-governmental organisations in international development*. London: Earthscan.

Gellner, Ernest (1981) *Muslim society*, Cambridge studies in social anthropology. Cambridge: Cambridge University Press.

—— (1994) *Conditions of liberty*. London: Hamish Hamilton.

—— (1995) 'The Importance of Being Modular', in John A. Hall, ed. *Civil society: Theory, history, comparison*. Cambridge: Polity Press, pp. 32–55.

Giddens, Anthony (1998) *The third way: The renewal of social democracy*. Oxford: Polity Press.

Glasius, Marlies, David Lewis and Hakan Seckinelgin, eds (2004) *Exploring civil society: Political and cultural contexts*. London: Routledge.

Göle, Nilüfer (1994) 'Toward an autonomization of politics and civil society', in Metin Heper and Ahmet Evin, eds. *Politics in the third Turkish republic*. Oxford: Westview Press, pp. 213–22.

Gordon, Ian, Janet Lewis and Ken Young (1977) 'Perspectives on policy analysis'. *Public Administration Bulletin* 25: 26–30.

Graziano, Paolo and Maarten Peter Vink, eds (2008) *Europeanization: New research agendas*. Basingstoke: Palgrave Macmillan.

Greenwood, Justin (2007) 'Organized civil society and democratic legitimacy in the European Union'. *British Journal of Political Science* 37(2): 333–57.

Grigoriadis, Ioannis N. (2009) *Trials of Europeanization: Turkish political culture and the European Union*. New York: Palgrave Macmillan.

Gunther, Michael M. (1989) 'Political instability in Turkey during the 1970s'. *Conflict Quarterly* 9(7): 63–77.

Hall, Peter A. and Rosemary C. R. Taylor (1996) 'Political science and the three new institutionalisms'. *Political Studies* 44(5): 936–57.

Hann, Chris M. and Elizabeth Dunn, eds (1996) *Civil society: Challenging western models*. London: Routledge.

Hayek, Friedrich A. von (1960) *The constitution of liberty*. London: Routledge and Kegan Paul.

Hegel, Georg Wilhelm Friedrich (1952) *Hegel's philosophy of right*. Oxford: Clarendon.

Heper, Metin (1985) 'Civil society and the state', *The State Tradition in Turkey*. Hull: Eothen Press, pp. 98–123.

—— (2002) 'Conclusion – The consolidation of democracy versus democratization in Turkey'. *Turkish Studies* 3(1): 138–46.

Hood, Christopher (1991) 'A public management for all seasons?' *Public Administration* 69(1): 3–19.

—— (1995) 'The "new public management" in the 1980s: Variations on a theme'. *Accounting, Organizations and Society* 20(2–3): 93–109.

Howell, Jude and Jeremy Lind (2009) *Counter-terrorism, aid and civil society before and after the war on terror*, Non-governmental public action series. Basingstoke; New York: Palgrave Macmillan.

Howell, Jude and Jenny Pearce (2001a) *Civil society and development: A critical exploration*. Boulder, CO: Lynne Rienner Publishers.

—— (2001b) 'Manufacturing civil society from the outside: Donor interventions'. *Civil society and development: A critical exploration*. Boulder, CO: Lynne Rienner Publishers, pp. 89–122.

Hulme, David and Michael Edwards (1997) *NGOs, states and donors: Too close for comfort?* Basingstoke: Macmillan in association with Save the Children.

Human Rights Watch (2008) 'Turkey: Court shows bias, dissolves Lambda Istanbul'. Available from http://www.hrw.org/en/news/2008/06/01/turkey-court-shows-bias-dissolves-lambda-istanbul. Accessed on 24 November 2008.

Ibrahim, Saad Eddin (1998) 'The troubled triangle: Populism, Islam and civil society in the Arab world'. *International Political Science Review* 19(4): 373–85.

Ishkanian, Armine (2008) *Democracy building and civil society in post-Soviet Armenia*, Routledge contemporary Russia and Eastern Europe series. London: Routledge.

Jalali, Rita (2002) 'Civil society and the state: Turkey after the earthquake'. *Disasters* 26(2): 120–39.

Jenson, Jane and Frederic Merand (2010) 'Sociology, institutionalism and the European Union'. *Comparative European Politics* 8(1): 74–92.

Jones, Steve (2006) *Antonio Gramsci*, Routledge critical thinkers. London; New York: Routledge.

Kadioğlu, Ayse (1996) 'The paradox of Turkish nationalism and the construction of official identity'. *Middle Eastern Studies* 32(2): 177–93.

Kalaycıoğlu, Ersin (2004) 'State and civil society in Turkey: Democracy, development and process', in B. Amyn Sajoo, ed. *Civil society in the Muslim world: Contemporary perspective*. London: I. B. Tauris, pp. 1–34.

Kamali, Masoud (2001) 'Civil society and Islam: A sociological perspective'. *European Journal of Sociology* 42(3): 457–82.

Kandiyoti, Deniz. A. (1987) 'Emancipated but unliberated? Reflections on the Turkish case'. *Feminist Studies* 13(2): 317–38.

Karaman, M. Lutfullah and Bülent Aras (2000) 'The crisis of civil society in Turkey'. *Journal of Economic and Social Research* 2(2): 39–58.

Karaosmanoğlu, Ali L. (1994) 'Limits of international influence on democratization', in Metin Heper and Ahmet Evin, eds. *Politics in the third Turkish republic*. Boulder, CO: Westview Press, pp. 117–31.

Kazamias, Geōrgios A. and Kevin Featherstone (2001) *Europeanization and the southern periphery*. London: Frank Cass.

Kazemi, Farhad (2002) 'Perspectives on Islam and civil society', in Nancy L. Rosenblum and Robert C. Post, eds. *Civil society and government*. Princeton, NJ: Princeton University Press, pp. 317–33.

Keane, John (1988) *Civil society and the state: New European perspectives*. London: Verso.

Keck, Margaret E. and Kathryn Sikkink (1998) *Activists beyond borders: Advocacy networks in international politics*. Ithaca, NY: Cornell University Press.

Keyman, Emin Fuat (1995) 'On the relation between global modernity and nationalism: The crisis of hegemony and rise of (Islamic) identity in Turkey'. *New Perspectives on Turkey* (13): 93–120.

Keyman, Emin Fuat and Ziya Öniş (2007) *Turkish politics in a changing world: Global dynamics and domestic transformations*. Istanbul: Istanbul Bilgi University Press.

Keyman, Fuat A. (2000) 'Global modernity, identity and democracy: The case of Turkey', in Günay Göksu Özdoğan and Gül Tokay, eds. *Redefining the nation state and citizen*. Istanbul: Eren, pp. 69–89.

Keyman, Fuat A. and Ahmet Icduygu (2003) 'Globalization, civil society and citizenship in Turkey: Actors, boundaries and discourses'. *Citizenship Studies* 7(2): 219–34.

Köker, Levent (1995) 'Local politics and democracy in Turkey: An appraisal'. *Annals of the American Academy of Political and Social Science* 540: 51–62.

Kösecik, Muhammet and Isa Sağbas (2004) 'Public attitudes to local government in Turkey: Research on knowledge, satisfaction and complaints'. *Local Government Studies* 30(3): 360–83.

Kubicek, Paul (1999) 'Turkish–European relations: At a new crossroads?' *Middle East Policy* 6(4): 157–73.

—— (2001) 'The earthquake, Europe and prospects for political change in Turkey'. *Middle East Review of International Affairs* 5(2): 34–47.

—— (2002) 'The earthquake, civil society, and political change in Turkey: Assessment and comparison with Eastern Europe'. *Political Studies* 50(4): 761–78.

—— (2005) 'The European Union and grassroots democratization in Turkey'. *Turkish Studies* 6(3): 361–77.

Kumar, Krishan (1993) 'Civil society: An inquiry into the usefulness of an historical term'. *The British Journal of Sociology* 44(3): 375–95.

Latour, Bruno (1986) 'The powers of association', in John Law, ed. *Power, action and belief: A new sociology of knowledge?* London: Routledge and Kegan Paul, pp. 264–80.

—— (1999) *Pandora's hope: Essays on the reality of science studies*. London: Harvard University Press.

—— (2005) *Reassembling the social: An introduction to actor-network-theory*, Clarendon lectures in management studies. Oxford; New York: Oxford University Press.

Lendvai, Noami and Paul Stubbs (2009) 'Assemblages, translation, and intermediaries in South East Europe: Rethinking transnationalism and social policy'. *European Societies* 11(5): 673–95.

Lewis, David (2001a) *Civil society in non-western context: Reflections on the 'usefulness' of a concept*. London: London School of Economics and Political Science.

—— (2001b) *The management of non-governmental development organizations: An introduction*. New York: Routledge.

Lewis, David and David Mosse (2006) *Development brokers and translators: The ethnography of aid and agencies*. Bloomfield, CT: Kumarian Press.

Long, Norman (2001) *Development sociology: Actor perspectives*. London: Routledge.

Lukes, Steven (1974) *Power: A radical view*, Studies in sociology. London: Macmillan.

Maina, Wachira (1998) 'Kenya: The state, donors and the politics of democratization', in Alison Van Rooy, ed. *Civil society and the aid industry: The politics and promise.* London: Earthscan, pp. 134–67.

Mardin, Şerif (1995) 'Civil society and Islam', in John A. Hall, ed. *Civil society: Theory, history, comparison.* Cambridge: Polity Press, pp. 278–300.

McLaughlin, Andrew M. and Justin Greenwood (1995) 'The management of interest representation in the European Union'. *JCMS: Journal of Common Market Studies* 33(1): 143–56.

Med-Pact (2009) *Technical assistance to the beneficiaries of the Med-Pact program.* Available from http://www.med-pact.com/Subpage.aspx?pageid=244&PID=153. Accessed on 9 July 2009.

Mercer, Claire (2002) 'NGOs, civil society and democratization: A critical review of the literature'. *Progress in Development Studies* 2(1): 5–22.

Ministry of the Interior (2010) *Local Administration Reform Programme: Introduction.* Available from http://www.lar.gov.tr/introduction.html. Accessed on 27 May 2010.

Mitlin, Diana (2004) 'Reshaping local democracy'. *Environment and Urbanization* 16(1): 3–8.

Mosley, Paul, Jane Harrigan and John F. J. Toye (1991) *Aid and power: The World Bank and policy-based lending in the 1980s, Vol. 2, Case studies.* London: Routledge.

Mosse, David (2004) 'Is good policy unimplementable? Reflections on the ethnography of aid policy and practice'. *Development and Change* 35(4): 639–71.

—— (2005) *Cultivating development: An ethnography of aid policy and practice,* Anthropology, culture, and society. London: Pluto Press.

Moussali, Ahmad S. (1994) 'Modern Islamic fundamentalist discourses on civil society, pluralism and democracy', in Augustus Richard Norton, ed. *Civil society in the Middle East, Vol. 1.* Leiden: E. J. Brill, pp. 79–119.

Müftüler-Baç, Meltem (2005) 'Turkey's political reforms and the impact of the European Union'. *South European Society and Politics* 10(1): 17–31.

Najam, Adil (1999) 'Citizen organizations as policy entrepreneurs', in David Lewis, ed. *International perspectives on voluntary action: Reshaping the third sector.* London: Earthscan, pp. 142–81.

Nozick, Robert (1974) *Anarchy, state, and utopia.* Oxford: Blackwell.

OECD (2008) *The Paris Declaration on Aid Effectiveness and the Accra Agenda for Action.* Available from http://www.oecd.org/dac/effectiveness/34428351.pdf. Accessed on 12 June 2010.

Öniş, Ziya and Fikret Şenses (2007) *Global dynamics, domestic coalitions and a reactive state: Major policy shifts in post-war Turkish economic development,* METU Studies in Development. Ankara: Middle East Technical University.

Open Society Institute (2007) *Soros Foundation Network Report 2007.* New York: Open Society Institute.

Ottaway, Marina and Thomas Carothers (2000) *Funding virtue.* Washington, DC: Brookings Institution Press.

Pace, Michelle, Peter Seeberg and Francesco Cavatorta (2009) 'The EU's democratization agenda in the Mediterranean: A critical inside-out approach'. *Democratization* 16(1): 3–19.

Pace, Roderick (2007) 'Clash of civilizations or intercultural dialogue? Challenges for EU Mediterranean policies', in Andrew Mold ed. *EU development policy in a changing world: Challenges for the 21st century*. Amsterdam: Amsterdam University Press, pp. 88–105.

Panayiotis, C. Ioakimidis (2001) 'The Europeanization of Greece', in Geōrgios A. Kazamias and Kevin Featherstone, eds. *Europeanization and the southern periphery*. London: Frank Cass, pp. 73–94.

Pamuk, Şevket (2008) 'Globalization, industrialization and changing politics in Turkey'. *New Perspectives on Turkey* (38): 267–73.

Parks, Thomas (2008) 'The rise and fall of donor funding for advocacy NGOs: Understanding the impact'. *Development in Practice* 18(2): 213–22.

Parla, Taha (1985) *The social and political thought of Ziya Gökalp, 1876–1924*. Leiden: Brill.

Polatoğlu, Aykut (2000) 'Turkish local government: The need for reform'. *Middle Eastern Studies* 36(4): 156–71.

Poulton, Hugh (1997) *Top hat, grey wolf and crescent: Turkish nationalism and the Turkish Republic*. London: Hurst & Company.

Putnam, Robert D. (1995) 'Bowling alone: America's declining social capital'. *Journal of Democracy* 6(1): 65–78.

—— (2000) *Bowling alone: The collapse and revival of American community*. New York: Simon & Schuster.

Putnam, Robert D., Robert Leonardi and Raffaella Nanetti (1994) *Making democracy work: Civic traditions in modern Italy*. Princeton, NJ: Princeton University Press.

Radaelli, Claudio M. (2004) 'Europeanisation: Solution or problem?' *European Integration Online Papers* 8(16). Available from http://eiop.or.at/eiop/pdf/2004-016.pdf. Accessed on 12 March 2009.

Rawls, John (1972) *A theory of justice*. Oxford: Clarendon Press.

Richter, James (2002) 'Evaluating western assistance to Russian women's organizations', in Sarah Elizabeth Mendelson and John K. Glenn, eds. *The power and limits of NGOs: A critical look at building democracy in Eastern Europe and Eurasia*. New York: Columbia University Press, pp. 54–90.

Risse-Kappen, Thomas (2001) 'A European identity? Europeanization and the evolution of nation-state identities', in Maria Green Cowles, James A. Caporaso and Thomas Risse-Kappen, eds. *Transforming Europe: Europeanization and domestic change*. Ithaca, NY: Cornell University Press, pp. 203–13.

Risse, Thomas, Maria G. Cowles and James A. Caporaso (2001) 'Europeanization and domestic change: Introduction', in Maria Green Cowles, James A. Caporaso and Thomas Risse-Kappen, eds. *Transforming Europe: Europeanization and domestic change*. Ithaca, NY: Cornell University Press, pp. 1–20.

Rubin, Barry (2002) 'Introduction – Turkey's political parties: A remarkably important issue'. *Turkish Studies* 3(1): 1–3.

Sajoo, B. Amyn (2004) 'Ethics in the Civitas', in B. Amyn Sajoo, ed. *Civil society in the Muslim world: Contemporary perspective*. London: I. B. Tauris, pp. 214–46.

Salamon, Lester M. (1981) 'Rethinking public management: Third-party government and the changing forms of government action'. *Public Policy* 29: 255–75.

—— (1987) 'Of market failure, voluntary failure, and third-party government: Toward a theory of government-nonprofit relations in the modern welfare state'. *Nonprofit and Voluntary Sector Quarterly* 16(1–2): 29–49.

Sandel, Michael J. (1996) *Democracy's discontent: America in search of a public philosophy*. Cambridge, MA: Belknap Press of Harvard University Press.

Sardan, J. P. Olivier de (1999) 'A moral economy of corruption in Africa?' *The Journal of Modern African Studies* 37(1): 25–52.

Scharpf, Fritz Wilhelm (1999) *Governing in Europe: Effective and democratic?* New York: Oxford University Press.

Schimmelfennig, Frank (2008) 'EU political accession conditionality after the 2004 enlargement: Consistency and effectiveness'. *Journal of European Public Policy* 15(6): 918–37.

Schimmelfennig, Frank and Ulrich Sedelmeier (2004) 'Governance by conditionality: EU rule transfer to the candidate countries of Central and Eastern Europe'. *Journal of European Public Policy* 11(4): 661–79.

—— (2008) 'Candidate countries and conditionality', in Paolo Graziano and Maarten Peter Vink, eds. *Europeanization: New research agendas*. Basingstoke: Palgrave Macmillan, pp. 88–101.

Seckinelgin, Hakan (2002) 'Civil society as a metaphor for western liberalism'. *Global Society* 16(4): 357–76.

—— (2004) 'Contractions of a socio-cultural reflex: Civil society in Turkey', in David Lewis, Hakan Seckinelgin and Marlies Glasius, eds. *Exploring civil society: Political and cultural contexts*. London: Routledge, pp. 173–80.

—— (2008) *The international politics of HIV/AIDS: Global disease-local pain*. London: Routledge.

Seufert, Günter (2000) 'The impact of national discourses on civil society', in Stefan Yerasimos, Günter Seufert and Karin Vorhoff, eds. *Civil society in the grip of nationalism*. Istanbul: Orient-Institut, pp. 25–47.

Simon, R. (1991) *Gramsci's political thought: An introduction*. London: Lawrence and Wishart.

Şimşek, Sefa (2004) 'The transformation of civil society in Turkey: From quantity to quality'. *Turkish Studies* 5(3): 46–74.

Smismans, Stijn (2003) 'European civil society: Shaped by discourses and institutional interests'. *European Law Journal* 9(3): 473–95.

Stetter, Stephan (2003) 'Democratization without democracy? The assistance of the European Union for democratization processes in Palestine'. *Mediterranean Politics* 8(2): 153–73.

Sunar, Ilkay (2004) *State, society and democracy in Turkey*. Istanbul: Bahçesehir University.

Sunar, Ilkay and Sabri Sayarı (1986) 'Democracy in Turkey: Problems and prospects', in Guillermo O'Donnell, Philippe C. Schmitter and Laurence Whitehead, eds. *Transitions from authoritarian rule: Southern Europe*. Baltimore: The Johns Hopkins University Press, pp. 165–186.

Tachau, Frank and Mary-Jo D. Good (1973) 'The anatomy of political and social change: Turkish parties, parliaments, and elections'. *Comparative Politics* 5(4): 551–73.

Tekeli, Sirin (1981) 'Women in Turkish politics', in Nermin Abadan-Unat, ed. *Women and Turkish society*. Leiden: E. J. Brill, pp. 293–310.

—— (1990) 'Women in the changing political associations of the 1980s', in Andrew Finkle and Nükhet Sirman, eds. *Turkish state, Turkish society*. London: Routledge, pp. 259–88.

Tocci, Nathalie (2005) 'Europeanization in Turkey: Trigger or anchor for reform?' *South European Society and Politics* 10(1): 73–83.

Today's Zaman (2009) 'DTP deputies to resign from Parliament after party closure'. 12 December.

Trägårdh, Lars (2007) *State and civil society in Northern Europe: The Swedish model reconsidered*, Studies on civil society. New York: Berghahn Books.

Tully, James (2002) 'Political philosophy as a critical activity'. *Political Theory* 30(4): 533–55.

Turkish Daily News (2007) 'NGOs issue their proposal for Article 301'. 9 February.

Turkish Statistical Institute (2010) *TurkStat*. Prime Ministry of Republic of Turkey 2010. Available from http://www.die.gov.tr/ENGLISH/index-english. html. Accessed on 16 December 2010.

TUSEV (2004a) *Comparative report on Public Benefit Law*, Available from http://www.icnl.org/news/2004/10-13TUSEVpublibenefitlawcomparativereport. doc. Accessed on January 24 2008.

—— (2004b) *Comparative report on Turkish Association Law Provisions*. Istanbul: TUSEV.

—— (2005) *Civil society in Turkey: An era of transition*. CIVICUS Civil Society Index Report for Turkey, TUSEV Publications No. 42, Istanbul: TUSEV.

—— (2008) *Civil Society Law Reform: Enabling civil society*. Available from http://www.tusev.org.tr/content/detail.aspx?cn=318&c=68. Accessed on 15 April 2009.

Tvedt, Terje (1998) *Angels of mercy or development diplomats? NGOs and foreign aid*. Trenton: Africa World Press.

Walzer, Michael (1983) *Spheres of justice: A defense of pluralism and equality*. New York: Basic Books.

Weiker, Walter F. (1990) 'The Free Party, 1930', in Metin Heper and Jacob M. Landau, eds. *Political parties and democracy in Turkey*. London: I. B. Tauris, pp. 83–98.

White, Gordon (1994) 'Civil society, democratization and development: Clearing the analytical ground'. *Democratization* 1(3): 370–85.

White, Jenny B. (2003) 'State feminism, modernization, and the Turkish republic woman'. *National Women's Studies Association Journal* 5(3): 145–59.

Wiltse, Evren Celik (2008) 'The Gordian Knot of Turkish politics: Regulating headscarf use in public'. *South European Society and Politics* 13(2): 195–215.

World Bank (2001) *Turkey Marmara earthquake assessment*. Ankara: World Bank Turkey Country Office.

Yavuz, M. Hakan (1999) 'Search for a new social contract in Turkey: Fethullah Gulen, the Virtue Party and the Kurds'. *SAIS Review* 19(1): 114–43.

—— (2003) 'Islamic social movements', *Islamic political identity in Turkey*. Oxford, New York: Oxford University Press, pp. 15–36.

—— (2009) *Secularism and Muslim democracy in Turkey*, Cambridge Middle East studies. Cambridge; New York: Cambridge University Press.

Yilmaz, Hakan (2006) 'Two pillars of nationalist euroskepticism in Turkey: The Tanzimat and Sevres Syndromes', in Ingmar Karlsson and Annika Strom Melin, eds. *Sweden and the European Union: Experiences and expectations*. Stockholm: Swedish Institute for European Policy Studies, pp. 29–40.

—— (2007) 'Islam, sovereignty, and democracy: A Turkish view'. *Middle East Journal* 61(3): 477–93.

Young, Iris (1993) 'Together in difference: Transforming the logic of group political conflict', in Judith Squires, ed. *Principled positions: Postmodernism and the rediscovery of value*. London: Lawrence & W., pp. 121–50.

Zürcher, Erik Jan (2005) *Turkey: A modern history*, 3rd edition. London: I. B. Tauris.

Index

Printed and bound in the United States of America